The Fun Guide to Walt Disney World®

FOR KIDS!

2024

Here you leave today—and visit the worlds of yesterday, tomorrow, and fantasy.

- Walt Disney

Published and distributed by Travel Made Easy (last update 11/21/2023).

Editor: Suzanne Albright

Contributing Authors: Jessie Sparks; Terri Miller; Melissa Moore

Cover Design: Suzanne Albright

Cover & Interior Art: Gary Bilodeaux

Retail Price: $19.99

Limit of Liability/Disclaimer of Warranty

The information in this book is subject to change and should be verified when making travel plans.

Information is published in a variety of electronic formats. Some content that appears in print may differ from that found in electronic books.

ISBN: 978-1-956532-09-8

Manufactured in the United States of America

10 9 8 7 6 5 4 3 2 1

Disney Trivia

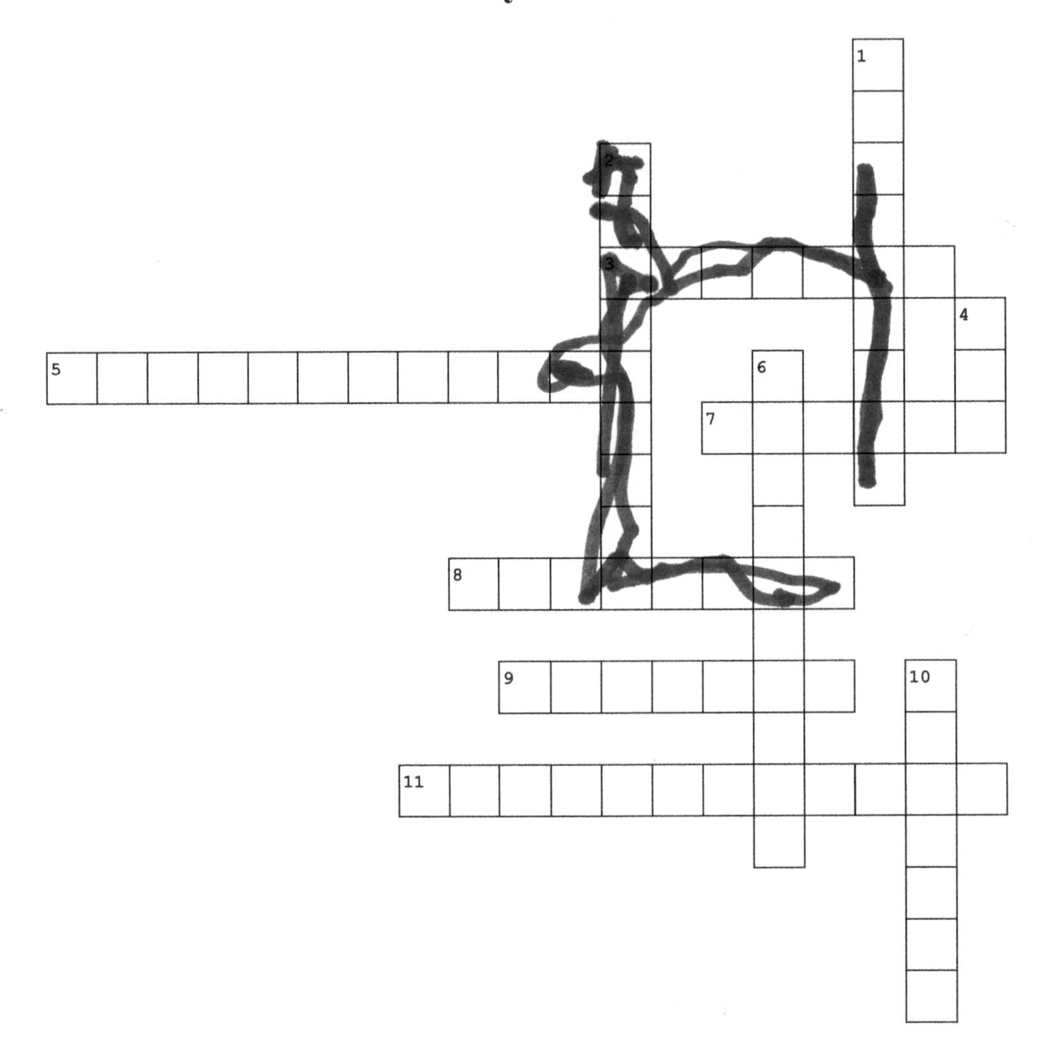

Across

3. In what month did Walt Disney World open?

5. Walt Disney World is about the same size as what city in California?

7. What is "Yen Sid" (the name of the sorcerer in Fantasia) spelled backwards?

8. In what month was Walt Disney born?

9. Who was Walt Disney's favorite U.S. President?

11. The first Walt Disney World theme park to open.

Down

1. Walt considered this Missouri city to be his home town.

2. Epcot stands for Experimental __________ Community of Tomorrow.

4. Walt's brother, friend and business partner.

6. The first Disney amusement park, opened in the 1950s.

10. In which state is Walt Disney World located?

*Answers on Page 211

Table of Contents

ANIMAL KINGDOM
OLLYWOOD TOWER
EPCOT

Recent Park Changes: What to Expect

(updated November 21, 2023)

READ THIS SECTION WITH YOUR PARENTS. IT'S REALLY IMPORTANT!

Crowds at the Parks

Disney World crowds are bigger than ever! This makes it feel very *congested* (meaning plugged up with people)! Tell your parents to expect some of the largest crowds ever seen at the parks this year. Will you be there?

Theme Park Operational Changes

Don't try to make last-minute plans. Walt Disney World Resort now requires an advanced reservation before entering any of the theme parks.

Your parents must buy tickets in *advance* (before your trip). Then they have to set up an account (either online or through the My Disney Experience app). Finally, they need to make a park reservation for every day of your trip.

You can still park hop, but it's different than it used to be. You need a reservation for the first park you visit each day. You don't need a reservation for the second park. The only problem is you may be turned away if that park is at *capacity* (meaning it's full). (You can check the app to see if the next park is available before hopping.)

FastPass+ reservations have been replaced with the paid Lightning Lane reservation system. (This is super important - read the Lightning Lane chapter!)

This means, if you don't pay for Disney's Genie+ day-of reservation system (Tier 2 attractions) or pre-reserve a paid time for Tier 1 attractions, you must wait in a *stand-by queue* for each attraction. Don't worry. We explain how all of this works later on in the book, so you can help your parents!

Cast Members (Disney employees) work hard to improve *efficiencies* (reducing wasted time). The lines may look long, but they usually move much quicker than you might think (and often quicker than the posted wait times).

Disney Transportation Changes

Disney transportation options are great, but they may have reduced *frequency* (meaning they don't run as often as years past). Because of this, plan an extra 15-30 minutes (depending on crowd size) to get somewhere if you're using any Disney transportation.

Security Screenings

Your family will go through a security screening when you enter each park and Disney Springs. If you have visited Walt Disney World before, you probably remember how that works. You walk through a metal detector, and a security guard might ask to check your backpacks, strollers, and other things for *prohibited* items (things you can't have in the parks).

Attractions, Shows & Character Greetings

Attractions and shows sometimes get refurbished or updated. They get shut down for a while when this happens. Have your parents check to make sure the shows and attractions you want to see are supposed to be open on your vacation dates.

Even if some are shut down, there's still lots to see. Kids especially love the *projection* or fireworks shows at each park.

Be sure to give your favorite character a big hug - and they will give you an autograph! There aren't as many character meet-and-greets as there used to be. The available characters also change. It's important to check the schedule to see which characters are at the park on the day you visit, so you don't miss out!

Don't worry if you can't meet all of them. You can also wave to your favorites in Character Processionals held throughout the parks.

Non-Theme Park Activities

Don't forget that Disney has a bunch of activities you can do on days you aren't going to a park. You can golf, rent boats, and even ride horses. (Read all about where to do those things in this book!)

Adults are only kids grown up, anyway.

- Walt Disney

Meet Mr. Walter Elias Disney

Walt Disney was born on December 5, 1901, in Chicago, Illinois. That's over 100 years ago! He grew up on a farm where he was taught the importance of hard work and learning new things.

As a young kid, Walt was very imaginative and loved to daydream. He would look up and pretend the clouds in the sky above were animals, with the wind changing their shapes from one farmyard critter to another.

From an early age, he wished to become a cartoonist. In his wildest dreams, he probably couldn't have imagined that he would become as famous as he did!

In 1928, Walt created a little black and white mouse cartoon character. At first, Walt wanted to name this mouse "Mortimer." His wife, Lillian Disney, didn't like that name and convinced Walt to name his mouse Mickey. That is how Mickey Mouse got his name!

Instant Animated Film Success. Mickey Mouse's first cartoon was *Plane Crazy*, a silent film. *Steamboat Willie* was the next cartoon Disney made. This second film is special because it was the first cartoon film to add *synchronized* sound that matched the action on the screen (called "synchronous sound"). This helped start a film revolution.

Walt's cartoons were very popular, and he *made a name for himself* (meaning he became well known).

Who were the Disney Brothers?

Walt and Roy Disney were close brothers since childhood, sharing a bed together on their family farm in Marceline, Missouri, where they spent their early years. They moved to Chicago when they were still both quite young.

Walt was always the creative dreamer. As he grew up, he developed skills as an artist and started drawing cartoons.

Roy always watched over his younger brother. When they were young, Roy would push his younger brother around in a baby carriage, as they walked the streets together. When they grew up, Roy's protective nature became especially important, as he helped Walt pursue his dreams.

The brothers worked together from early on. In 1923, when Walt was only 21, the two co-founded the Disney Brothers Studio, and this relationship eventually evolved into the Walt Disney Company. Roy became a great businessman and ran the business. He worked easily with early investors and corporate partners. Roy once said, "My job is to help Walt do the things he wants to do."

Walt knew he couldn't succeed without his brother, who was his greatest supporter. To capture how important Roy's support of Walt was, there is a special bench in Town Square of Magic Kingdom with statues of Roy and Minnie Mouse sitting on it. These are the two unsung heroes in the world of Disney, playing important supporting roles to Walt and Mickey Mouse.

Snow White and the Seven Dwarfs

Disney's big hit came in 1937 with the full-length movie (also called *feature film*) *Snow White and the Seven Dwarfs*. If you have not yet seen this animated movie, it is fun for everyone in the family!

Walt became a world-famous movie producer. His first movies were cartoons. He also broke ground in "live-action" (which is a fancy way of saying they use real actors). Some of his productions included both **cartoons and live-action characters**, like Mary Poppins. Disney's skill at combining both types of films set the company apart in the industry.

Theme Park Developer. It was a full 30 years after his first film before Walt built his first theme park, Disneyland. As you may know, this is located in Anaheim, a city near Los Angeles, in southern California.

Where Did the Idea for a Theme Park Originate? Family was important to Walt. One Saturday, Walt took his wife and two daughters to an amusement park. His two young daughters loved the trip, but he felt the park was simply not clean or nice enough.

Walt was also discouraged at the lack of fun rides and other things parents could do with their children. He thought, "I wish there were a place where children and grown-ups could have fun together."

Mr. Disney and his brother became inspired and knew they could create a better

Grimm Fairy Tales

Did you know *Snow White* is a tale from German folklore that dates all the way back to 1812? It was first written down by a couple of brothers, named Grimm. Disney was heavily influenced by their stories, which can also be seen in other movies.

Many people think Snow White may is based on a real German royal named **Maria Sophia Margaretha Catharina, Baroness von und zu Erthal**, who was born in 1725!

"The idea for Disneyland came about when my daughters were very young and Saturday was always Daddy's day with the two daughters. So we'd start out and try to go someplace, you know different things, and I'd take them to the merry-go-round and I took them different places and as I'd sit while they rode the merry-go-round and did all these things -- sit on a bench, you know, eating peanuts—I felt that there should be something built where the parents and the children could have fun together.

So that's how Disneyland started. Well, it took many years...it was a period of maybe fifteen years developing. I started with many ideas, threw them away, started all over again. And eventually it evolved into what you see today at Disneyland. But it all started from a daddy with two daughters wondering where he could take them where he could have a little fun with them, too."

~ Walt Disney

and cleaner place for families. In fact, Walt made a rule that trash cans would be no more than 30 paces apart to make it easy and convenient for guests to throw away trash. Every person working at the park is required to pick up garbage they find as they walk about the park.

Kid's Trivia!

Chewing gum isn't sold anywhere on Disney property, because kids have a habit of spitting it out on the ground or sticking it under their seat!

There is a statue of Walt with Mickey Mouse in front of the Cinderella Castle at the Magic Kingdom. It's called the *Partners Statue*. The plaque on it talks about his dream:

Partners. We believe in our idea: A family park where parents and children could have fun - together.

~ Walt Disney

"When I started Disneyland, my wife used to say, 'But why do you want to build an amusement park?' They're so dirty,' I told her that was just the point – mine wouldn't be."

~ Walt Disney

Disney Characters

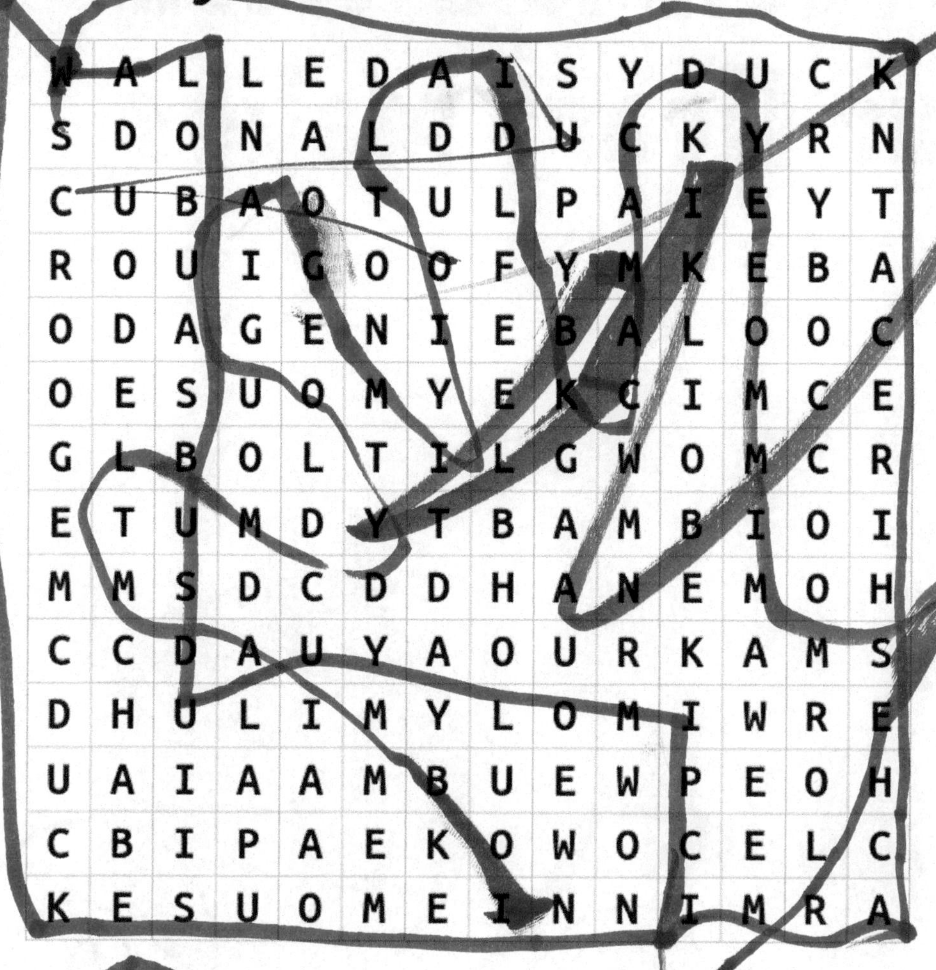

NEMO
GOOFY
CHIP
DAISY DUCK
BOLT
MICKEY MOUSE
PLUTO
BALOO
THUMPER
DONALD DUCK
MINNIE MOUSE
CHESHIRE CAT
SCROOGE MCDUCK
WALL-E
WOODY
DALE
DUMBO
BAMBI
MOWGLI
ARIEL
GENIE
ABU

A Dream is a Wish Your Heart Makes

Important Dates in Disney History

JULY 17, 1955—DISNEYLAND OPENS IN ANAHEIM, CALIFORNIA

For years, Walt dreamed of the ideal place where grown-ups and kids could play together. It took him a long time to convince his brother, Roy, that they could make it work. It was going to cost a LOT of money, more money than the brothers could ever imagine—and more than the banks wanted to let them borrow. Walt and his brother had to risk everything they had worked for in order to build their theme park.

Fears of going broke haunted them, since they were striving for something bigger and better than anyone had tried before! However, at no point in time did the brothers give up on their dream!

Great success made Walt dream even bigger! After Disney's success with the Disneyland theme park and animated films, Walt dreamed of making his entertainment empire even greater. What he started would soon grow into a *fabulously huge* company.

He decided to open a new and much larger park somewhere where the weather was always warm, and close to where a lot of people in the United States lived. For this reason, he chose Orlando, Florida.

Walt Disney died December 15, 1966. While plans were made, work had not actually begun on the first Disney World theme park: Magic Kingdom. Roy believed in Walt's dreams and kept them alive. He honored his brother by naming the property the **Walt Disney World Resort**. Sadly, Roy died on December 20, 1971, just two-and-a-half months after the Magic Kingdom opened.

Did you know? Over 20 million people travel to the Magic Kingdom each year—it's the most popular theme park in the world!

In 1955, Disneyland opens in Anaheim, California. Walt makes a dedication speech at the grand opening of the family park and says, "Here age relives fond memories of the past, and here youth may savor the challenge and promise of the future."

The park becomes a blockbuster success with millions of visitors from all over the world.

KID'S TRIVIA!

Disneyland was initially going to be called Mickey Mouse Park.

The Walt Disney Company Today

The Walt Disney Company is one of the world's largest companies in the entertainment and information business. It even owns several television channels, including ABC (American Broadcasting Company), ESPN, and Freeform. You probably watch these channels all the time and never realized they are owned by Disney.

The Walt Disney Company is known for its amazing movies and great TV shows. They create tons of products to go with those movies and shows, like books, toys, clothes and even apps for your phone. Disney is everywhere!

GUEST
RELATIONS
CAST

Disney History

Do you want to learn even more about Walt Disney?

Visit *Walt Disney Presents* located at Disney's Hollywood Studios. There is more fun information than you could imagine in this museum and show. If you think you're a Walt whiz, ask for a Citizenship Test from the Cast Member at the exhibit hall's entrance. After passing the test, you become an Honorary Citizen of Disney World. You even get a special certificate!

Important Dates in Disney History

1901	December 5—Walt Disney is born in Chicago, Illinois
1928	First "synchronized sound" Mickey Mouse cartoon, *Steamboat Willie*
1937	First full-length animated film, *Snow White and the Seven Dwarfs*
1955	Disneyland Park in Anaheim, California opens
1971	October 1—Magic Kingdom park opens near Orlando, Florida
1975	The first Magic Kingdom roller coaster, *Space Mountain*, opens
1982	October 1—Epcot park opens
1983	Tokyo Disneyland opens (In Japan's capital city)
1989	May 1—Disney-MGM Studios opens (now Disney's Hollywood Studios)
1992	Disneyland Paris opens (in France's capital city)
1996	Disney World's 25th anniversary
1998	April 22—Animal Kingdom park opens (Earth Day)
2006	Expedition Everest opens in Animal Kingdom's Asia
2008	Toy Story Mania! opens in Disney's Hollywood Studios
2011	50th Anniversary of Walt Disney World Resort
2012	Disney purchases the Lucasfilm company (Star Wars) for $4 billion
2016	Star Wars expansion begins
2016	Frozen Ever After Attraction opens in Norway pavilion in Epcot
2017	Pandora world opens in Animal Kingdom
2018	Toy Story land opens in Disney's Hollywood Studios
2019	Star Wars: Galaxy's Edge land opens in Disney's Hollywood Studios
2020	Mickey & Minnie's Runaway Railway opens in Disney's Hollywood Studios
2021	Disney World's 50th anniversary
2023	The Disney Company's 100th anniversary

Your Walt Disney World Trip!

Kid's Tip!

Take notes as you read through this book to help remember important things. Write down the name of each attraction and show you want to see.

HINT: When you see this ***Kid's Tip!*** icon, it means one of our readers shared important information with us.

Here are a few things kids really love
Meeting Disney Characters
What you need to know

If you are reading this book, it probably means one thing...You are planning a very special trip…

You're going to Walt Disney World!

Disney World is "the most magical place on Earth" and the absolute best place for kids! It is also great for families because it lets out the hidden child within every adult - everyone can play and have a blast!

Disney World is WAY MORE than just an amusement park. Most kids have been to a state or county fair and think that Disney World is about the same size and has the same number of fun things to see and do. A county or state fair is not even close!

Did you know? Disneyland in Anaheim, California, is known as "The Happiest Place on Earth."

Take any one you have ever been to and multiply the fun and excitement by 100!

This book tells you about everything you need to know to become an expert on all things Disney. It's filled with awesome advice from kids just like you!

Orlando is called the "City Beautiful." It is a large city where you can soak up the sun pretty much all year round.

Disney World is a huge town with a ton of stuff to do.

Disney World is located in the heart of Central Florida, in the southwest region of Orlando, Florida.

From Interstate 4 (I-4), look for the many Walt Disney World exits. Just tell your folks to follow the signs!

Use the maps in this book and these directions to help your parents get there.

If your parents are driving south, take Interstate 95 (I-95), US Route 1 or the Florida Turnpike southbound until reaching I-4. Then, travel westbound on I-4 into the Orlando area, until you see the signs for Disney.

If you're heading east (from the Tampa area), tell your parents to start the journey on Interstate 75 (I-75), until you reach I-4.

Oswald the Lucky Rabbit was created by Walt Disney and Ub Iwerks in 1927 for Universal Pictures.

If your parents are driving north (from south of Orlando), have them take the Florida Turnpike to the Kissimmee-St. Cloud exit and follow (State) Highway 192 (Irlo Bronson Memorial Highway) to the west until reaching Walt Disney World.

Remember to look for the signs. Don't miss it!

You are going to have so much fun experiencing amazing amusement rides and seeing live stage shows. You can also meet many Disney Characters, like Mickey Mouse himself!

Did you know? Disney World is an actual CITY the size of San Francisco, California. It is twice the size of Manhattan Island in New York. *Really!* What's more, Disney World even has its own government, firefighters and paramedics!

Everyone here wants to help you have a fantastic vacation filled with happy family memories! Read along and let us help you plan a perfect trip.

We know this is a big book. You don't have to read it all. Skim it now really fast to find what you like the most. Pick it up

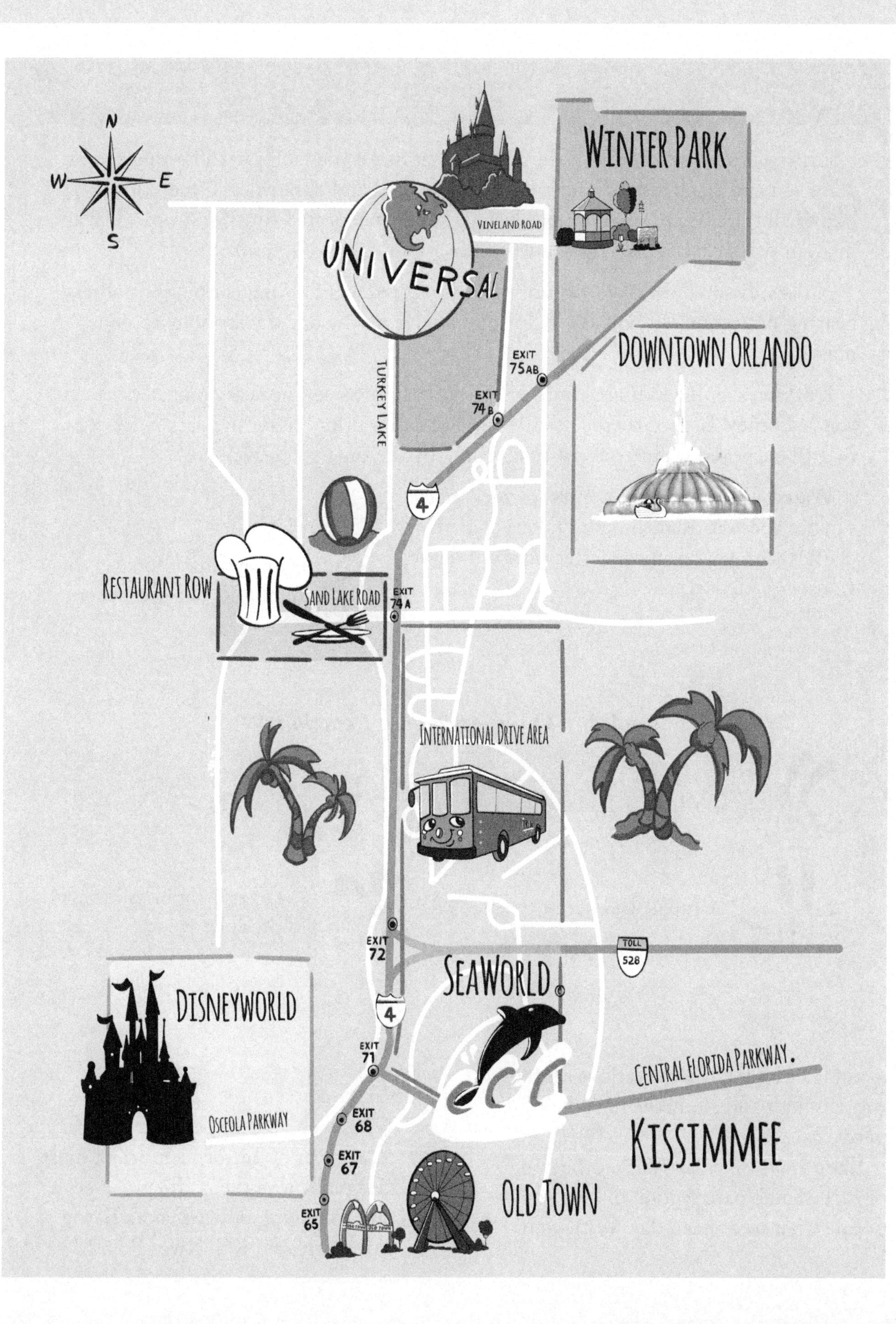
N
W
E
S
WINTER PARK
UNIVERSAL
VINELAND ROAD
DOWNTOWN ORLANDO
EXIT 75AB
EXIT 74B
TURKEY LAKE
4
RESTAURANT ROW
SAND LAKE ROAD
EXIT 74A
INTERNATIONAL DRIVE AREA
EXIT 72
TOLL 528
SEAWORLD
DISNEYWORLD
4
EXIT 71
CENTRAL FLORIDA PARKWAY.
EXIT 68
OSCEOLA PARKWAY
KISSIMMEE
EXIT 67
OLD TOWN
EXIT 65

Surprises!

Surprises come in all forms, from things that make you laugh to those that might scare you ever so slightly. Some kids don't like loud and dark rides. Other kids don't like thrill rides where you go super-fast and take unexpected turns or drops. (If your mom or dad's back is bad, they must be careful on fast rides, too!)

Noises. If you don't like loud noises, ask your parents to bring ear plugs or other hearing protection. (It will also help you nap during the day if your hotel room is noisy!)

Darkness. Some kids are afraid of the dark. Remember, no scary monsters can get you at Disney! In fact, there's usually a ton of fun waiting inside the dark rides. You may be surprised to find out you're laughing by the time you leave!

Water. There are also a couple of rides that can get you wet. Remember to take a change of clothes with you, or those water rides will leave you soggy all day!

Kid's Tip!

Bring an eye mask to keep the light out of your eyes when you sleep.

Look for These *Attraction Reactions*™!

	Thrills & Excitement!		You May Get **Soaked**!
	A Little Scary!		Dizzy/Motion Sickness Possible!

again later to read those sections all the way through and study the most helpful parts.

Keep Lists. We have lists at the end of each theme park section to help you decide what to do each day. With your

Kid's Tip!

Even though Expedition Everest and Tower of Terror seem scary, most kids really love them. They also get a thrill plunging down Tiana's Bayou Adventure and Kali River Rapids!

Kid's Tip!

Take this book on your trip with you. Remember to pack it in your luggage! You can glance back through it when you visit each park so you don't miss a thing. It also gives you something to look at while you wait in lines.

list, you can keep track of everything you don't want to miss.

Even if a wild ride looks scary—don't worry! You're completely safe. Disney adds a lot of fun special effects and makes sure there's no real danger. Just remember it's all make-believe. Just like all the action and scary stuff you see on television and at the movies, nothing here is real – except for the fun! Think of it like a big movie set.

Let your inner daredevil come out to play!

Here are a few things kids really love:

Slinky Dog Dash and the Indiana Jones Epic Stunt Spectacular at Hollywood Studios;
Test Track and Remy's Ratatouille Adventure at Epcot;
Peter Pan's Flight and Tiana's Bayou Adventure at Magic Kingdom; and
Kilimanjaro Safaris and Flight of Passage at Animal Kingdom.

Meeting Disney Characters

Character Meet and Greets, Photographs and Autographs. Take time to meet all your favorite characters and get their autographs! Bring your autograph book and a big pen, because the characters have big hands. (Some of them have a hard time holding skinny pens.)

If you have a camera, be sure to take it! Otherwise, ask your parents to snap the shots that YOU are going to want to share with your friends when you get home. Your parents can also buy pictures from Disney's PhotoPass system. These are photos taken by professional Disney photographers and automated camera systems in all the best spots, including the coolest rides!

Let's Learn about Characters!

A character is a real-life version of the animated creatures and people in Disney movies and television shows. Although these characters may appear very small in film, they are actually as big as grown-ups!

There are two different kinds of characters: known as **Face** and **Fur**.

Face Characters. These look a lot like regular people and include Princesses, Princes, Peter Pan, Mary Poppins, and even Alice in Wonderland, to name a few.

Kid's Tip!

Don't forget to smile on the rides. Disney takes photos of you on a lot of them! On the rides that take automatic pictures or video, there is a preview area where you can see your photo right after you hop off the ride. Make sure to stop by and see how you looked. They can be really funny sometimes!

They are called face characters because you can see their faces and talk to them.

Fur Characters. Fur characters are mostly animals. These include some of your favorite characters, such as the "**Fab 5**" (*fab* is short for fabulous): Mickey, Minnie, Goofy, Donald and Pluto. Fur characters love big hugs, but they do not talk. Instead, they use gestures to communicate – kind of like sign language, but easy for everyone to understand!

Character Meet & Greet Schedules. Character Meet and Greets are at scheduled times and places. They take a picture with you and sign autographs if you bring something to write on.

Find Character Greeting times in the Times Guide at each park's Guest Relations or at the Guest Information Desk (concierge desk) if you're staying at a Disney hotel. If you have additional questions, ask your hotel Cast Member to check the Character Hotline (only available at a Disney hotel) to see when and where a character is available.

What you need to know:

TRIP LENGTH: Seeing all the important stuff at Walt Disney World takes at least five or six full days inside the parks, and that's not counting all the other stuff to do in Orlando.

Even if you can only visit the Florida sun for a few days, it is still better than no fun at all. Some families can plan a once-in-a-lifetime trip that lasts two full weeks, while others stay only four or five days at a time.

There is no perfect length for a Disney World vacation; what is right for some is not right for others. If your family can afford a longer stay, try to plan at least a week to 14 days – especially if it is your first trip!

It is so big that you need way more than a single day to see and do everything. But even if you can only come for a day or two, you can immediately start planning your next trip to catch everything you missed!

Did you know? Trips to Walt Disney World Resort should take at least a week. This has been voted the best length of stay for a family vacation!

There are tons of really cool things to do and see at Walt Disney World. No matter how long your stay is, it's nearly impossible to do it all, and that's not even counting all the other stuff in Florida.

As you go through this book, think about what you really want to make sure you see or do. Talk to your family, too. Everyone will have their own ideas. Work together to come up with a good plan to make everyone happy.

HINT FOR CHAMPIONS! The early bird really does get the worm at Disney. This is no time to be lazy. Get up early! Aim to arrive at the parks *before* opening! Sleep in and you may miss out on the best rides. Plan on being the one that gets the rest of your family to rise out of bed in the mornings!

It's not advertised, but the Magic Kingdom lets you enter Main Street (the shopping area) 60 minutes before its official opening time; the other parks allow you inside between 10 - 30 minutes early. The rides aren't actually running yet, but this lets you get to your first adventure quickly! Plus, if you get to the Magic Kingdom early, you can see an awesome opening show that only a few people see each day.

Opening Time. Parks usually open at 8:00 a.m. or 9:00 a.m.

Closing Time. Parks stay open until 9:00 p.m. or 10:00 p.m., but some stay open past midnight on really busy days!

Check Operating Hours. Ask a parent to check the hours ("operating hours") for each theme park on the day your family is planning to visit. Remind them that this information is on the My Disney Experience app, or they can ask at the Guest Information desk at the hotel.

Early Theme Park Entry (Replaced Extra Magic Hours). This special *perk* (short for "perquisite" meaning *bonus*) is available only to guests staying at Disney hotels. You are let into a park 30 minutes before everyone else each day. Even better, you get to choose the park.

As a special perk, Disney hotel guests are sometimes allowed to stay late in a park. That means you get extra time to enjoy all those rides with shorter lines! Try not to miss these extra hours if you can help it.

Plan where you're going to eat before you go!! Tell your parents they can save a lot of time by making lunch and dinner reservations for popular restaurants before you go on your trip. They can reserve dining times as early as two months (60 days) before your trip. You can even meet some of your favorite Disney friends, like Mickey and Minnie, when you eat at some of the really nice places. This means you won't have to wait in line to see them at the parks!

Minimum Height on Attractions

Do you know how tall you are? We know you're really excited about all the rides. Some rides are made just for big kids, though.

That means you have to be tall enough for some attractions. In other words, there is a minimum height required for some bigger rides.

Get your measuring tape out and ask a parent to help you figure out your height. You can compare it with the following list to see if you are tall enough for the big kid stuff.

We know it can be disappointing if you're a little too short to go on that really awesome attraction. Just remember, it's to keep you safe. You wouldn't want to slip out of a harness and fall! Plus, you can use it as a reason to go to Disney World when you're a couple of years older!

It's not all bad news if you're too little for some rides. The two water parks each have attractions designed only for children, so the height requirements keep bigger kids and adults away!

Here are rides with minimum height requirements for each park:

Magic Kingdom

- The Barnstormer: 35in (89cm)
- Big Thunder Mountain Railroad: 40in (102cm)
- Tron Lightcycle Power Run: 48in (122cm)
- Seven Dwarfs Mine Train: 38in (95cm)
- Space Mountain: 44in (113cm)
- Tiana's Bayou Adventure: 40in (102cm)
- Tomorrowland Speedway: 32in (82cm)

Epcot

- Guardians of the Galaxy: Cosmic Rewind: 42in (107cm)
- Mission: SPACE: 44in (113cm) for Orange or 40in (102cm) for Green
- Soarin': 40in (102cm)
- Test Track: 40in (102cm)

Hollywood Studios

- Rock 'n' Roller Coaster: 48in (122cm)
- Star Tours: 40in (102cm)
- Star Wars: Rise of the Resistance: 40in (102cm)
- Slinky Dog Dash: 38in (95cm)
- The Twilight Zone Tower of Terror: 40in (102cm)
- Millenium Falcon: Smugglers Run: 38in (95cm)

Animal Kingdom

- Avatar Flight of Passage: 44in (113cm)
- DINOSAUR: 40in (102cm)
- Expedition Everest: 44in (113cm)
- Kali River Rapids: 38in (95cm)

Typhoon Lagoon

- Bay Slides: 60in (152cm) or shorter. That's right! This limitation benefits the kids.
- Crush 'n' Gusher: 48in (122cm)
- Humunga Kowabunga: 48in (122cm)
- Ketchakiddee Creek: 48in (122cm) or shorter. One just for the kids!

Blizzard Beach

- Chairlift: 32in (82cm)
- Downhill Double Dipper: 48in (122cm)
- Slush Gusher: 48in (122cm)
- Summit Plummet: 48in (122cm)
- Tike's Peak: 48in (122cm) or shorter. Another kids only attraction!

Attraction Height Requirements

Minimum Height	Magic Kingdom	Epcot	Hollywood Studios	Animal Kingdom	Minimum Height
54"	Tomorrowland Speedway	*Note:* Must be 32" to ride with an older driver.			54"
48"	Tron Lightcycle Power Run		Rock 'n' Roller Coaster		48"
44"	Space Mountain	Mission: SPACE (Orange Team)		Expedition Everest	44"
				Avatar Flight of Passage	
42"		GOTG Cosmic Rewind			42"
40"	Tiana's Bayou Adventure	Soarin'	The Twilight Zone Tower of Terror	DINOSAUR	40"
	Big Thunder Mountain Railroad	Test Track	Star Tours - The Adventures Continue		
		Mission: SPACE (Green Team)	Star Wars: Rise of the Resistance		
38"	Seven Dwarfs Mine Train		Slinky Dog Dash	Kali River Rapids	38"
			Millenium Falcon: Smugglers Run		
35"	The Barnstormer				35"
32"	Tomorrowland Speedway	*Note:* Must be 54" to ride alone.	Alien Swirling Saucers		32"

Planning Your Trip is Fun!

We know you like reading. How? Because this book is in your hands! Maybe you're someone who loves writing and drawing pictures about Disney World. (We'd love to see your art and read your stories, too! Feel free to send them to us after getting your parent's permission. You may see them in a future edition!)

A lot of our readers love playing sports, using a computer, singing, dancing and making music, too. Most of us like watching live shows where we can sing along to our favorite songs.

Did you know that you can do all of these things at Disney World?

Are you someone who likes taking photographs and shooting videos? There are a lot of picture opportunities to uncover while you explore. Don't forget all the wildlife you will get to see in their natural habitats at the Animal Kingdom.

Photo Spots. Disney PhotoPass photographers are at some of the coolest locations in the parks, but there are lots of other great spots to take photos. Look for "Photo Spot" signs to find great places to get a memorable snapshot.

Sports. Some kids like golf, and other kids like mini golf. There are lots of great golf courses in Walt Disney World, including regular, mini and even footgolf! There's even one mini golf course that's a shrunk-down, pro golf course, complete with real grass! There are also tennis and basketball courts at some of the hotel resorts, if that's your type of sporting fun.

ESPN Wide World of Sports. Kids who really love sports are going to love the ESPN Wide World of Sports complex. This area has been hosting sports competitions and welcoming sports fans of all kinds for about 20 years.

It is a huge property, spanning 230 acres, with 10 tennis courts and a track and field arena. The complex also holds a whopping 9,500 spectators in its Champion Stadium baseball park. This is where the Atlanta Braves baseball team holds its Spring Training camp!

If you spot a bunch of teenagers walking around the parks wearing sports, cheer or dance uniforms, they are probably

Planning Your Trip is Fun!

Kid's Tip!

If you like to run, every Disney resort has an outdoor running track that will show you a map and tell you how far you can run. Just look for the signs that say "New Balance Running Trail." This can be a fun and healthy way to explore your resort.

Kid's Trivia!

Did you know a full marathon is 26.2 miles? That's a lot of running! Disney often holds half marathons (13.1 miles) and sometimes even shorter runs. The word *marathon* comes from a Greek legend. Pheidippides was a hero who ran all the way from the village of Marathon to Athens to announce that they had won a battle. The distance was about 26.2 miles. Poor Pheidippides collapsed and died right after making the announcement!

attending a competition at ESPN. In fact, during November, ESPN has big cheer competitions, and the Pop Warner Football league comes to play championship games.

Marathons. If you want a fun but physical challenge, try running a marathon at Disney! Disney hosts themed running events throughout the year (rundisney.com) that take you from one park to the next. Some of them are just for kids, like the ***run*Disney** Kids Races.

Fishing and Boating. Some kids really like fishing with Mom and Dad, or boating with the entire family. Disney has several places to do both.

In addition, there are water sports activities just a couple miles away from Disney Springs, on Lake Bryan. Buena Vista Watersports is a lakeside watersports company that's easy to get to if you are staying near Disney World. It offers something for everyone in your family, including paddle boarding, kayaking, jet skiing, and other water fun! Ask your parents to look up **Buena Vista Watersports** on State Highway 535, just south of Interstate 4 (I-4)! Disney World also offers some of these fun water sports at different resorts. You don't need to be staying at the resort to do them, either. They are available for anyone to do, so long as your parents agree to pay for it.

Water Parks. Later in this book, we tell you all about Disney World's two water parks, where you can spend all day splashing around under the hot, Florida sun.

Hotels

Kids especially like the great themes at Disney resorts, such as Art of Animation. It has an awesome underwater music pool and giant-size replicas of some of your favorite Disney movie characters. At Caribbean Beach Resort, you can go on an actual pirate ship cruise with other kids (no parents allowed!). Animal Kingdom Lodge lets you see many real, live animals, and Fort Wilderness has horses and acres of wilderness to explore. Read more about these cool experiences and more in our section about resort hotels towards the end of this book.

Treats! Of course, you're going to love all the tasty treats that Disney offers, including churros, Mickey Mouse ice cream bars, popcorn, and the famous soft, frozen pineapple ice cream treat called a *Dole Whip*. It's yummy!

Meals. Look for the section in this book that shares lots of food choices kids love!

Favorite Rides Lists. At the end of each park section, we have a table that lists all the must-see rides and attractions. Of course, pretty much everything at Disney is a kid-pleaser! Our list just lets you know which rides you should put first on your list, so there is no chance you are going to miss them. Make sure you look over these tables!

Attraction Refurbishments. Disney sometimes shuts down rides to make repairs. If a ride is important to you, ask an adult to check for it on the list of scheduled maintenance at the following website: www.wdwinfo.com/wdwinfo/rehab.htm.

Meeting the Characters. You can spend days just meeting your favorite Disney stars, but don't get so caught up that you miss out on the rides and shows. Pick only two or three characters to meet at each park to give plenty of time for other fun stuff.

Live Performances. Singing. Dancing. Action. You get everything at the stage shows in Hollywood Studios and Animal Kingdom. Don't forget to see shows like *Nemo* and *Fantasmic*! (We'll tell you more about these later.)

Getting Ready for Disney Fun!

Ask a parent to help you figure out what the weather in Florida should be like when you visit. Pay special attention to the season in which you're traveling to Walt Disney World.

Florida is usually extra warm and humid (that means you feel hot and sticky), but it can get very chilly any time in the late fall through early spring (especially November to February). Even if the day is warm, it can cool down at night. Don't forget to take along a warm jacket and sweater if you visit in these months, *just in case.*

It can both rain very hard and get sizzling hot on the same summer day. During this season, the weather can get wild. It can really pour (but luckily, it doesn't usually last too long)! The thunderstorms are often intense with a lot of lightning. If you see lightning nearby, get under cover.

Kid's Tip!

Bring an umbrella or poncho if the weather report gives a 40% or greater chance of rain. You can keep enjoying the parks, while everyone else runs for cover!

A poncho is very easy to fold up and put away when the rain clears up. It will also help keep you dry on the water rides! (Tell your parents to buy ponchos at a dollar store before your vacation starts—the ponchos in the parks are pretty pricey!)

Summer Heat Warning. It gets really hot at least half the year in Florida. Pay attention when you are playing in the sun. It is important to note if you stop sweating. This is a serious sign that you are overheated. Keep an eye on your parents and siblings to watch for these warnings, too.

- Keep drinking water <u>even when you don't feel thirsty</u>. Take a break every 20 minutes for a long sip on hot summer days.
- There is an increased risk if you run around a lot.
- If you start to feel faint, lightheaded or dizzy, tell an adult!

Hurricane season. Hurricanes are pretty rare in Central Florida, although Walt Disney World had to shut down for hurricanes in both 2016 and 2017! If one does happen, the airport stops allowing flights to come to the city, so you don't have to worry about flying into Orlando during one. If you are already at Disney World when a hurricane hits, Disney will make sure you are safe and taken care of. "Hurricane season" is the period from June 1 to November 30 - peaking from late August through September. (September 10th is the "statistical peak" of the hurricane season – meaning it's the most likely day to have one.)

Getting Ready for Disney Fun!

Packing Your Luggage. Leave packing to your parents. Just double check that they bring:

- Sunscreen and bug spray – a painful sunburn ruins your vacation, and no one likes to scratch bug bites.
- Shorts and pants. Opt for shorts unless you are visiting in December, January or February.
- Long and short-sleeved shirts, sweaters and jackets.
- Lightweight clothing and comfortable shoes that you can spend a lot of time walking in. They should be well-worn in. Do not bring brand new shoes, no matter how cute or cool they are. It's easy for feet to get blisters, and these are no fun.
- Bathing suit (one piece for girls – some rides can rip away tops)!
- Hat and sunglasses.
- A favorite Disney costume, such as a princess or pirate costume, to dress as a favorite character at the park!

Clothing. Wear layers if it might get cool, like sweaters and jackets over your T-shirt. When you wear layers, it means that as you warm up, you can take off one piece of outer clothing. Since you keep them with you in a backpack, when it starts to cool down in the evening, you can put the layers back on to warm up.

Plan & Pack Like A Pro!

Tell your parents to download and use our free planning and packing tools at:

bit.ly/DisneyPlanners

There's a Packing Checklist, Budget Worksheet, Attraction Planner, and Dining Planner - and they don't cost a penny!

Fun In the Sun Warning!

Remember to Use Sunscreen and Wear Sunglasses!

Sunscreen. Make sure to use lots of sunscreen and reapply throughout the day! This is especially important for people from the northern states and those with fair skin, but anyone can get burned if they are not careful.

Did you know? As much as 80% of the sun's rays get through the clouds on a hazy day. You need protection if you are spending any time outside, not just when you go to the beach. Ultraviolet (UV) rays from the sun can burn the skin, leaving you in pain and misery during your trip. If your parent asks, tell them to get a Sun Protection Factor (SPF) of at least 30, including what is called "Broad Spectrum."

Please remember that it only takes 15 to 30 minutes for your skin to burn if it is not protected by clothing or sunscreen. Because the lotion does not last all day, you will need to put more on every couple of hours, and even more often if you are playing in a pool.

It is important to wear sunglasses to protect your eyes. If you play in the water, glare from the sun is even more dangerous to our young eyes.

Kid's Tip!

Don't Forget! Ask your parents for dark sunglasses and a hat with a wide brim. The Florida sun is super bright!

Kid's Tip!

Leave room in your suitcase for souvenirs you can take home with you!

Kid's Tip!

Ask your parents nicely for a brand new Disney T-Shirt as soon as you get to the park. Better yet, have them buy you one before you go. It'll cost less money and be a fun thing to wear as you travel to Disney!

Lightning Lanes & Genie+

Remind Your Parents about Lightning Lanes!
Rider Switch (Child Swap)

Did you know you can reserve a time to go on some of your favorite attractions? Disney has a reservation system that lets you walk to the front of the line for most attractions.

With a reservation, you get on a ride almost as quick as lightning. That's why Disney named the special *queues* for people with reservations *Lightning Lanes*!

Lightning Lane reservations cost money. Check with your parents to see if they want to pay extra money to save time or use that money for other things.

If your parents don't get Lightning Lane reservations scheduled for popular rides, you have to go through the regular line (called the *standby queue* – pronounced just like the letter "Q"). This can take a lot more time, so be prepared.

The best option is to get your family to the park really early in the morning. Otherwise, just keep an eye on the line throughout the day to see when wait times are low!

Kid's Tip!

Use the My Disney Experience app to see when the wait times to get on a ride are low. The app is great for ordering food, reserving Lightning Lanes, checking out showtimes and lots of other things. For really popular rides, you might have to wait for a parade or the fireworks to see wait times go down.

The best Lightning Lane reservations run out fast, so you have to hurry!

The reservation system is confusing. Most adults don't understand it, so your parents may need your help!

There are two different reservation systems: *Genie+* or *Individual Lightning Lane* reservations. How you make and pay for a reservation depends on how popular the ride is.

Look at it this way. Some attractions are so popular, people wait for hours to go on them. We call those Tier 1 attractions. Brand new rides and shows are often Tier 1.

Other rides are still fun, but the wait time for them is usually under one hour. We call those Tier 2 attractions. A lot of *oldie-but-goody* rides are Tier 2, including *Peter Pan's Flight* and *Soarin' Around the World*, but a lot of the new rides are also on this list!

There are also Tier 3 attractions. These are the ones you can usually walk right on with almost no wait. *Swiss Family Robinson Tree House* and *Carousel of Progress* are good examples of Tier 3.

Tier 3 attractions don't have Lightning Lanes available. You can't reserve a time to visit them, because you don't need to!

Tier 2 attractions are part of the Genie+ reservation system. You can pay $15 or more per person for the Genie+ (*Genie Plus*) service each day of your vacation.

Let's say you're going during a busy time and the per person cost is $27. If there are four people in your family,

Genie+ costs at least $108 per day.Genie+ every day!

That can really add up if you use Genie+ every day! Fortunately, you can choose to use it (or not) for as many days as you want. Your parents may only want to pay for Genie+ if the park is super busy, like Magic Kingdom usually is.

There are usually two Tier 1 attractions at each park. You can't reserve Tier 1 attractions through Genie+. To get on a Tier 1 ride quickly, you need an Individual Lightning Lane reservation.

Individual means you need to pay for a separate reservation for each popular ride you want to do. In other words, if you want to go on Tron Lightcycle Power Run, each person must pay money for just that single ride.

Some Tier 1 attractions are more popular than others. Also, a park might be busier on one day and slower on another. Because of this, there may be more or less people trying to go on a Tier 1 ride.

Disney changes the amount they charge for Individual Lightning Lane reservations each day. If it's a really busy day and a really popular ride, you pay more. If you go to Disney during a slow season (meaning less people are traveling), you pay less.

Each Individual Lightning Lane reservation costs anywhere from $7 to $20 per person. That's a lot of money.

Make sure your parents know to include it in the trip *budget*. (The budget is how much money your family has available to spend on the vacation.)

Using Disney's Genie

Most people just call it "Genie." However, you may sometimes hear it called "Genie *Plus*." They mean almost the same thing.

Genie is the free portion of the service. Genie+ is the part you have to pay to use.

With Genie, you can make an *itinerary* for each day of your trip. The itinerary is a list of things you want to do each day.

Genie makes it super easy. Genie is part of the My Disney Experience app, so make sure your parents download it! (You can probably help your parent(s) set up the app!)

Use Genie to choose the calendar day and the park you're visiting. After that, simply answer a few questions about your likes and dislikes.

Genie will automatically create a suggested itinerary. You can select an item on the itinerary to change it if you don't like something.

Once you have the itinerary, Genie makes suggestions for Genie+ and Individual Lightning Lane Reservations. Your parents can simply click a button on the app to start reserving rides!

Kid's Tip!

Disney also changes it them park ticket prices based on the same system. That means a trip to Disney costs less when less people can go, like when you're in school. It costs more when lots of people want to go, like during summer break!

Learn About Virtual Queues!

Disney sometimes uses virtual queues for brand new rides, like *Tron Lightcycle Run*. Rather than stand in a line, you sign up to enter the queue *virtually* through the My Disney Experience App.

Virtual queues open at 7:00 am each morning and fill up right away. If you don't get a spot in a virtual queue, there is no standby queue.

The only other way you can go on that attraction is to pay for an Individual Lightning Lane reservation!

Tell your parents they have to wait until the morning of each park visit to make reservations for Genie+ or Individual Lightning Lane attractions.

They can make the first Tier 2 reservation as early as 7:00 a.m. the morning of your visit. You can't do it before that time!

Each time you use a Genie+ reservation, you can make a new reservation through the app.

You can only have one Genie+ reservation at a time. Also, you can't reserve the same attraction more than once per day.

It's a little different for Tier 1 attractions.

You can only buy two Individual Lightning Lane Reservations per day. This means you have to choose which two of the most popular you want to do for every day of your trip.

Just like with Genie+, you must wait until the day of your visit to make a Tier 1 reservation.

If you're staying at a Disney hotel, you can reserve your Tier 1 Lightning Lane times as early as 7:00 a.m.

If you're staying off-property (at a non-Disney hotel), you have to wait until the park opens for the day to make a Tier 1 Lightning Lane reservation.

Because Tier 1 rides are so popular, that means all the reservations might be sold out by the time the park opens!

Rider Switch (Child Swap)

If you have a younger brother or sister who is too scared or too small to go on any ride, you are in luck! Disney has a way to make sure all of the adults get a turn to go on the ride, and it means the older kids get to go on it twice!!!

What is Rider Switch? You and your folks simply meet the queue attendant and ask to do the "Rider Switch." The Cast Member counts the number of kids in the party and gives the adults in the group a paper pass. This allows one or more parent (or other adults) to take the older kids on the ride, while the other waits with the younger kid(s). Then, when you're done riding the first time, the waiting adult can use the pass to take all the bigger kids on the ride a second time!

If some Tier 1 rides are really important for your family, make sure your parents know. They may decide to stay at a Disney hotel to make sure you get all the Lightning Lane reservations you want!

The scheduled time lets you show up to the ride or attraction any time over an hour-long period of time, or "window." For example, if your Lightning Lane reservation is 1:05 p.m. to 2:05 p.m., you can arrive anytime in that window.

- **Hint:** There is a "grace period" for most Lightning Lane reservation windows; you can show up 5 minutes early or arrive 15 minutes late and may still be admitted to the attraction.

After reading this book, think about which rides and attractions you absolutely HAVE to see. Then, ask your mom or dad to reserve Lighting Lanes times for them.

Kid's Tip!

If a stay in a Disney hotel doesn't fit the trip budget, tell your parents they can book just one or two nights of your vacation in one of them.

You can still get all the perks for those days, including early booking of Lightning Lane reservations!

LET US HELP! Here is a list of the rides and attractions you may want to consider. They are the Must-See rides for which we think you really need Lightning Lane reservations. A star next to the name means it's a really popular attraction. Two stars means it's one of the most popular rides and very high in demand!

Lightning Lane Recommendations

Magic Kingdom

- ★ Peter Pan's Flight
- ★★ Seven Dwarfs Mine Train
- ★ Enchanted Tales with Belle
- Buzz Lightyear's Space Ranger Spin
- Tomorrowland Speedway
- ★ Tiana's Bayou Adventure
- ★ Space Mountain
- Pirates of the Caribbean
- Big Thunder Mountain Railroad
- ★★ Tron Lightcycle Power Run (opening later in 2022)

  NOTE: Tron does not have a standby queue. If you don't get a Lightning Lane reservation, the only way to ride is through the virtual queue. Sign up for it at 7:00 a.m. in the app!

Magic Kingdom has 15 attractions we rate **Must-See** (see the end of the Magic Kingdom section). They all have Lightning Lanes available. The ones on the list above are favorites among kids.

Just remember, there are tons of rides at the Magic Kingdom. Because there are so many things to do at this park, it is impossible to see them all unless you are visiting the park for two or more days.

Epcot

- Mission: SPACE
- Spaceship Earth
- ★★ Frozen Ever After
- ★★ GOTG: Cosmic Rewind
- ★ Test Track
- ★ Soarin' Around the World
- ★★ Remy's Ratatouille Adventure

Epcot has 11 attractions we rate **Must-See** (see the end of the Epcot section).

Disney's Hollywood Studios

- ★★ Mickey & Minnie's Runaway Railway
- ★ The Twilight Zone Tower of Terror
- ★★ Slinky Dog Dash
- ★ Toy Story Mania
- Alien Swirling Saucers
- Fantasmic!
- ★ Rock 'N' Rollercoaster
- ★ Millennium Falcon: Smugglers Run
- ★★ Rise of the Resistence

Hollywood Studios has 12 attractions we rate **Must-See** (see the end of the Hollywood Studios section).

Disney's Animal Kingdom

- ★★ Avatar Flight of Passage
- ★ Kilimanjaro Safaris
- Festival of the Lion King
- Expedition Everest

Animal Kingdom has nine attractions we rate **Must-See** (see the end of the Animal Kingdom section).

Kid's Tip!

Starting later this year, Disney will include free downloads of attraction photos for each day you buy Genie+.

It costs about $17 to download a single attraction picture without Genie+. The per day cost of Genie+ starts at $15 per person and goes up from there. (It is more expensive on busy days.)

Your parents can buy a Memory Maker Package for $199 that includes downloads of every picture taken on your vacation. (It's only $169 if you buy it before your trip!)

Help your parents do the math to see if Memory Maker or Genie+ is a better value.

Hidden Mickeys

Disney "Imagineers" are the people behind the scenes who design all the fun. The job title combines the words "imagination" with "engineering."

What are Hidden Mickeys?

Description

Search for the classic 3-circle Mickey silhouette.

The so-called "classic design" uses three circles to represent Mickey's face and large, round ears. This is the most basic and standard kind of Hidden Mickey, but there are other kinds. A Hidden Mickey could also be:

- a detailed image of his ears and face (or body).
- a 3-D representation.
- a profile: Mickey may appear as a side profile (often showing only 3/4) of his face, head and ears. It may also be as a full side profile of his body.
- a full-length silhouette of him from the front.

Sometimes Hidden Mickeys include just his handprints, gloves, shoes, or ears. Even finding his initials or name in unexpected locations could be a Hidden Mickey. (Though very rare, other Disney characters are also "hidden," including Minnie Mouse, Donald Duck, Goofy and others.)

Discover Hidden Mickeys in the shadows or lights, in gemstones, rocks and trees. Look up to the sky murals painted on ceilings and perhaps see a Hidden Mickey cloud. At night, you might find one in the fireworks as they explode in the sky. They can be found in any type of drawings or decoration, as well as walls, murals and wood carvings.

Hidden Mickeys are meant to be discrete or secret. When you notice one, it will be in a random place that surprises you. They have been "hidden" intentionally and integrated into design elements in a way that would not otherwise be expected.

Imagineers have hidden more than 250 Mickey ears and silhouettes in unexpected places throughout Walt Disney World just for you to find! It's like a fun treasure hunt to try to find them all.

What Hidden Mickeys are NOT. While often found in plain sight, a Hidden Mickey is not a regular Mickey drawing, like something printed on a sign or restaurant's menu. You can't claim anything used in promotional advertising.

- A Hidden Mickey is also not the shape you see in a sign or shop window display where the symbol would be expected.
- It is not decorative placements in windows, walls or gates.
- Likewise, it is not the obvious markings on manhole covers or other such construction designs.

Hidden Mickey Etiquette

Proper etiquette means that you should always be considerate of Cast Members and other guests. If you are searching in a line, move out of the way and let other guests pass you. Having manners requires that you don't interrupt another guest in line, at a restaurant or anywhere else without asking permission first.

If you let those around you know what you are doing, they may join in to help you look. They may have never heard about Hidden Mickeys!

Here are a few Hidden Mickey locations to get you started:

The Haunted Mansion. Look for the two saucers and a plate at the bottom of the table in the ghost party room.

Buzz Lightyear Space Ranger Spin. Look inside the building where there is a poster on the right wall. The continents on Planet Prime form Mickey! During the short movie, watch the planets as they fly by. About halfway through the space video scene, you'll see a Hidden Mickey speed past.

Tomorrowland Transit Authority PeopleMover. Look on the belt of the lady you see getting her hair done after passing by the Metro Retro Society.

Carousel of Progress. More than one can be found in the Christmas scene. Look at the top of the fireplace mantle to see a Mickey nutcracker.

it's a small world! Look for some in the Africa room, in the purple leaves on the ceiling and others near the giraffes.

Disney is like Alice stepping through the looking glass; to step through the portals of Disney will be like entering another world.

- Walt Disney

Disney Villains

A	M	A	L	E	F	I	C	E	N	T	Y	R	T
L	I	H	R	A	T	I	G	A	N	Z	R	N	O
U	A	E	F	R	O	L	L	O	A	S	G	E	R
S	E	R	G	A	R	C	A	O	H	A	I	Y	A
R	N	O	K	O	A	E	D	O	R	A	Z	N	F
U	R	R	K	I	B	A	I	R	B	M	N	R	A
S	E	D	A	H	N	A	K	L	A	A	N	S	J
Y	I	D	H	A	K	G	N	A	I	G	A	R	C
T	C	K	O	Y	A	O	C	R	A	C	U	F	L
F	Z	A	S	C	A	R	S	A	E	D	A	T	A
G	G	A	S	T	O	N	Y	Y	N	H	N	F	Y
E	F	U	Y	N	A	H	S	H	K	D	C	G	T
N	H	A	K	E	R	E	H	S	F	E	Y	L	O
C	S	Y	N	D	R	O	M	E	E	R	S	S	N

SYNDROME
FROLLO
SHERE KAHN
JAFAR
FACILIER
GASTON
SHAN YU
HANS
KAA
HADES
MALEFICENT
RATIGAN
CHERNABOG
SCAR
KING CANDY
CLAYTON
SYKES
YZMA
URSULA

Walt Disney World is a Real City Filled with Awesome Fun

Did you know that Disney World is the size of the entire city of San Francisco, California? (If you don't know where this is, it is a city by the Pacific Ocean in Central California.)

Disney World is huge! It is hard to describe it, and it will cause you to go "Wow!" when you see it all!

Summary

Magic Kingdom (1971)

Cinderella Castle sits in the hub (center) of the park with six lands surrounding it.

Main Street, U.S.A. is the first land you see. The other lands you encounter are Adventureland, Liberty Square, Frontierland, Fantasyland and Tomorrowland.

Kid's Trivia!

Even though the Magic Kingdom looks a lot like Disneyland in California, there are quite a few differences. For instance, Disneyland has two more lands: New Orleans Square and Critter Country!

Epcot (1982)

Epcot is split into four parts, three that explore science and industry (World Celebration, World Discovery, and World Nature) and another that celebrates the cultures of countries throughout the world (World Pavilion).

The front half of the park is devoted to science and discovery. This is where most of the rides are located. In World Showcase, you can become an international explorer as you tour 11 countries across the globe, sampling authentic food and experiencing the culture, architecture and attractions of each country pavilion.

World Nature includes a gigantic aquarium filled with all kinds of fish and even sharks. This is where The Seas with Nemo and Friends is found. As you continue through this area, you won't want to miss the realistic hang gliding adventure of Soarin' Around the World. In this ride, you "fly" over tons of beautiful and famous sights in the world, while feeling the wind in your hair and smelling the aroma of each area. Every kid's favorite character, Figment, also has his own ride in World Celebration! Journey with him into imagination. You won't believe the amazing things you see!

World Discovery has probably the coolest (and busiest) ride of all. Help the Guardians of the Galaxy save our world on *Cosmic Rewind*. It's one of the longest indoor roller coasters in the world!

While most of the rides are in the front half of the park, there are a few in World Showcase. In fact, two of Epcot's most popular rides are in Norway and France. The *Frozen Ever After* attraction takes you on a boat ride through Anna and Elsa's frozen Norwegian homeland.

For a really zany experience, shrink to the size of a rat and take a spin on *Remy's Ratatouille Adventure*.

Remember reading about Lightning Lane reservations? You are definitely going to want Lightning Lane reservations for them. They are super popular. Both kids and adults want to experience them, so they always have a really long line!

Here is the order of the country pavilions as you walk around World Showcase in a clockwise manner (turning left at the end of the walkway, as you enter World Showcase).

- Mexico
- Norway
- China
    - African Outpost—This is a small area that is not a pavilion but a beverage and souvenir retail location. It is influenced by Africa and has an authentic feel.
- Germany
- Italy
- United States of America (American Adventure)
- Japan
- Morocco
- France
- The United Kingdom
- Canada

Take your time and explore each country. Some of them have hidden mini-rides inside of them (go into the pyramid in Mexico), movies to enjoy, performances to watch, really fun shopping and other experiences, like museums!

Disney's Hollywood Studios (1989)

This park celebrates show business and the magic of movie-making! You'll be amazed at the stunts performed in the *Indiana Jones Stunt Spectacular.* If you're into Star Wars, be sure to sign up for Jedi Training - you'll be a part of the show! You might even get to fight Darth Vader himself!

Beauty and the Beast – Live on Stage. This is a fan favorite! If you liked the movie, you'll love this live stage show. The real performers bring this great story, literally, to life!

Twilight Zone Tower of Terror. This is the definitely the most awesome *drop ride* in the world. Disney set the standard for this type of fun, and you will not be disappointed!

Rock 'N' Roller Coaster. This is one of the most exciting roller coasters at Walt Disney World. It has loop-de-loops and is made to look like its traveling at night on a winding highway! This coaster takes off and speeds up from 0 to 60 miles per hour in just a couple seconds. It drives like you wish Grandpa would!

Toy Story Mania. This 4-D shooting game stars your favorite Toy Story characters. The whole family will love riding through a midway-like area and blasting up things to score points.

Slinky Dog Dash. Get ready to zoom along on the back of Toy Story's Slinky Dog. This tame roller coaster is made especially for kids!

Alien Swirling Saucers. Hang on to your hat as one of Toy Story's aliens tows you around inside a giant claw machine. It's so fun to zip around in giant circles!

KID'S TRIVIA!

Disney purchased the *Star Wars* franchise in 2012. They built an entire Star Wars land called Galaxy's Edge in Hollywood Studios that opened in 2019. It's out of this world!

Millennium Falcon: Smugglers Run. Become an international space smuggler as you pilot the galaxy's fastest space ship!

Star Wars: Rise of the Resistance. Take on the First Order in an epic battle with the Resistance.

Disney's Animal Kingdom (1998)

The famous icon of this park is the giant tree at its center - *The Tree of Life*. Be sure to walk on the **Discovery Trails** around the tree—look for over 300 animal carvings within the trunk of the tree! There are also animal habitats to find tucked into these walkways—that's why they're called *Discovery* trails.

The best thing about the tree, for kids, is the special 3-D (three dimensional) movie housed in an underground theater in the roots. *It's Tough to Be a Bug!* is the title of the movie, which is about the life of bugs and how they help humans. The movie uses special "bug vision" glasses so the bugs look like they're coming out of the screen towards you. (*It's Tough to Be a Bug!* is actually considered a 4-D movie because it adds other special effects like sprinkles of water, scents and creatures in the theater, too.)

Oswald the Lucky Rabbit was created by Walt Disney and Ub Iwerks in 1927 for Universal Pictures.

Disney's Animal Kingdom is also known for having the *coolest* thrill roller coaster at Disney World. It is called **Expedition Everest**. In this ride, you get to take an exciting and exhilarating ride to the top of a snow-capped mountain where the giant Yeti, or abominable snowman, is waiting for you!

Probably the thing that kids like most is the number of live animals they get to see. It is the only park where the main theme represents nature, wild animals and conservation – in a super-fun way!

Real Animals! You can take an authentic African safari ride, called *Kilimanjaro Safaris*, where you drive by the homes of lions, giraffes and other wild animals. Next door to the safari ride, walk through exhibits where you see more birds and bats than you could ever count, along with a family of gorillas.

In another walk-through exhibit (next to Kali River Rapids), there's a family of Asian tigers!

An Alien Adventure. *Pandora* is an alien landscape brought to life straight from the *Avatar* movie. Possibly the best ride in the world is here, *Flight of Passage*. Using some of the most advanced technology, you are genetically synched (linked) with an avatar to take a flight on the back of a banshee. You will swear you're actually flying around Pandora!

Dinosaurs. If you like these prehistoric creatures, don't miss *Dinoland USA*! If your parents want a little break, but you're still wanting to explore—check out the *Bone Yard*! It's a playground-adventure area where you can run, excavate in the sand and discover!

Do you want the thrill of being with Dinosaurs? Head over to the ride called *DINOSAUR*, hop aboard a Time Rover and come face-to-face with the biggest and fiercest dinosaurs ever!

Typhoon Lagoon and Blizzard Beach Water Parks

Disney has two water wonderlands that all kids love. The size of these parks is totally out-of-this-world! They set the standard, and they are awesome choices for kids' fun.

Slip down water slides, float on water rafts and relax in cool pools. There's no better way to spend a hot Florida day. Want to chill even more? Take a soothing float once or twice around the lazy river - both waterparks have one!

Kid's Tip!

Of both parks, most kids like Blizzard Beach the best. It has conveyor belts for the inner tubes, so you don't have to carry them up a bunch of stairs.

The water parks are a great way to escape from a busy day at the theme parks. Get wet and stay cool during the hottest part of the day - the afternoon! This is usually when the regular theme parks are most busy, too.

REMEMBER! Kids under ten need an adult with them when they visit a water park.

Disney's Typhoon Lagoon

Resort Pools

Lots of Orlando hotels have great pools. Some even rival the water parks with fun stuff to do!

If you're staying at a Disney hotel, you know their top-notch resort pools are great. Value resorts usually have fun themes for their water play areas, but Moderate to Deluxe resorts also have water slides at their pools!

More Water Fun!

Disney has a few fun fountains where you can get really wet. If you plan to play in the water, don't forget to bring a change of clothes or wear a swimsuit underneath your regular clothes. That way, you can get

Disney's Blizzard Beach

super soaked at Tiana's Bayou Adventure in Frontierland or at the Casey Jr. Splash and Soak Station in Storybook Circus (Fantasyland) and dry off quickly after!

There are a few other areas, such as water splash zones at Epcot and Disney Springs where kids can splash around to cool down, play and have a lot of fun!

Other fun things to do around Disney include:

- Boats
- Miniature golf courses
- Bikes
- Horses
- Parades
- Fireworks
- Meeting characters!

Things change all the time and throughout the year, so no matter how often you get to visit Disney World, there are new things to see and experience. Disney never disappoints!

Planning is half the fun! Help your parents start planning early. It usually takes at least **three** months to take care of all the details! Here are some things you can help decide:

- Which parks should you visit?
- When is the best time of year to go?
- What clothing should you pack?
    - Remember: if you want to play in the water at one of the parks, your parents are going to have to pack extra clothing to keep dry ones with you!
- Which characters can you meet and where can you find them?
- Which attractions do you want to experience?
- Are there special restaurants you want to try?

WRITE IT DOWN! Get out note paper and a pencil to take notes! Make a plan!

There are more than 300 attractions at Disney World! This means that you need to create a schedule, so you don't miss what matters to you.

Keep adding notes and then write out your master list when you are ready

to leave home. Start with four sheets of paper, one page for each of the major parks. Write the name of one park at the top of each page. When you read about something that you want to do, write it down on the appropriate piece of paper.

Kid's Tip!

Use *Post-it* notes, if you can. They let you move things around without having to rewrite your notes.

When you are finished, pick your top five "must see" attractions and then number the rest of the attractions in order of importance.

Afterwards, review your notes, print the schedule found on the first page of the appendix (at the back of this book) and rewrite your choices on it.

Share this final list with the other kids who are traveling with you to make sure you can agree on what to do. Then, share your plans with your parents (or whichever adult is taking care of things). They need it so that they can complete their vacation planning (like getting reservations to your favorite restaurants!) and scheduling your Lightning Lane reservations.

After all the reservations have been made, print your final schedule (called an itinerary). Give a copy to everyone who is traveling with you.

Kid's Tip!

Ask your parent to take a picture of your itinerary with their smart phone in case anyone loses their printed copy!

Children never get lost at Disney! Disney is the only place that understands that it is not kids that get lost, but our parents!

If you ever get separated from your family (It's easy to do with all the things to see and do!), find any Disney employee. (Disney employees are called Cast Members – look for a Disney name tag to tell if it's a Cast Member.)

Tell them your family is lost and needs help finding you. They put all their efforts into finding your folks quickly, so you can get on with your fun.

To make sure everyone is easy to find, have your parents take a picture of you and your brothers and sisters each morning. If they find a Cast Member, they can show them what you look like and what you're wearing - this can help speed up the process of reuniting everyone!

Kid's Tip!

Ask your parents to write down their cell phone numbers on something you won't lose (like your arm). You can show it to the Disney Cast Member if you get separated. They can call your parents for you!

Disney Trivia!

Did you know that Walt Disney didn't like people pointing with their index fingers? He thought this action looked rude. This is why Cast Members are taught to use a "**Disney point**" with both the index finger and middle finger, together. They can also indicate direction with their entire hand opened. This gesture is called an "open-palm" point. Try it!

Did you know? Everything is controlled at the park, including sights, sounds and even smells. Disney pumps air into each "land" area to make sure the entire experience is immersive (meaning you are completely surrounded by it, so nothing from the outside world is there).

Playing at the Parks!

Final Hints for your Visit!
Things that Fright & Things that Excite!

Before you get to the theme parks, download the Play Disney Parks app. It opens up a whole new world of fun for you, which changes based on where you are! For instance, the app becomes a Galactic Datapad when you arrive at Star Wars: Galaxy's Edge in Hollywood Studios. You can scan objects, listen in on communications and even translate what you're saying to an alien language. Try it in each land of each park to see what fun you can discover!

The parks have so much to do, we could never describe all of it. We're going to try, though! Here is a table that lists the total number of shows, rides and games. You can see that the Magic Kingdom has the most to do, by far!

Shows and Rides

Park Name	Number of Shows	Total Rides	Interactive Games
Magic Kingdom	15	27	0
Epcot	16	10	1
Hollywood Studios	14	8	0
Animal Kingdom	15	9	1

If you can dream it, you can do it.

- Tom Fitzgerald, Disney Imagineer

Parades

Park	Parade Name
Magic Kingdom	Festival of Fantasy; Move It! Shake It! Dance & Play It!
Epcot	None
Hollywood Studios	None
Animal Kingdom	None

Note: Parades are often referred to by the time they occur, e.g., the three-o'clock parade.

Shows

Here is a table that lists all the shows. Read through the names to decide which ones sound interesting.

Park	Show Name
Magic Kingdom	Let the Magic Begin Country Bear Jamboree The Hall of Presidents Enchanted Tales with Belle Mickey's PhilharMagic Monsters, Inc. Laugh Floor Walt Disney's Carousel of Progress Main Street Trolley Show Disney Enchantment Flag Retreat The Dapper Dans Casey's Corner Pianist Mickey's Royal Friendship Faire Once Upon a Time The Royal Majesty Makers
Epcot	Disney & Pixar Short Film Festival Turtle Talk With Crush O Canada! Entertainment at Canada Mill Stage Reflections of China Impressions de France Beauty & The Beast Sing-A-Long The American Adventure British Revolution Harmonious JAMMitors Jeweled Dragon Acrobats Mariachi Cobre Matsuriza Serveur Amusant Voices of Liberty

Hollywood Studios	Beauty and the Beast Live on Stage Disney Movie Magic Fantasmic! For the First Time in Forever: A Frozen Sing-Along Celebration Indiana Jones Epic Stunt Spectacular Jedi Training: Trials of the Temple Lightning McQueen's Racing Academy March of the First Order Muppet* Vision 3D Star Wars: A Galactic Spectacular Star Wars: A Galaxy Far, Far Away Star Wars Launch Bay Theater Wonderful World of Animation
Animal Kingdom	It's Tough To Be A Bug! Bollywood Beats Burudika Donald's Dino-Bash! Feathered Friends in Flight Festival of the Lion King Finding Nemo – The Musical Hakuna Matata Time Dance Party Kite Tails Pandora Rangers Swotu Wayä Na'Vi Drum Ceremony Tam Tam Drummers of Harambe Tree of Life Awakenings Viva Gaia Street Band! Winged Encounters – The Kingdom Takes Flight

Final Hints for your Visit!

Relax and Chill!

If you go to a park early in the morning, plan to take a break in the afternoon when the weather is the hottest and the parks are the most crowded. This is the best time to go back to your hotel and play in the pool or take a cat nap.

When you return later in the afternoon, you can go on a lot of the rides again. It will be cooler and not as busy.

Some of the outdoor rides are really fun after it gets dark, like Big Thunder Mountain Railroad!

If you get tired, most of the parks have fun ways to rest your feet. At Magic Kingdom, take the train around the park or hop aboard the PeopleMover. Animal Kingdom also has a great train ride, and Epcot has boats. If you are lucky, you will get a cool breeze!

Stage Fright! *"Exit stage right!"*

Don't worry if you get nervous waiting in line for a ride and "chicken out" at the last second. This happens to a lot of us at any age! There are exits before you get on the any ride at Disney that you can take without having to hang your head in shame. Just remember that the rides aren't actually dangerous or really scary when you get on them. They're all super fun!

Motion Sickness!

Be careful about the rides you take right after eating. Some of them can make you feel sick, especially if you have a sensitive stomach. If you ever get car sick, this may be you. So, be careful with the following rides if you're worried about getting motion sick.

Magic Kingdom

- Mad Tea Party
- Seven Dwarfs Mine Train
- Space Mountain
- The Barnstormer
- Big Thunder Mountain Railroad
- Tron Lightcycle Power Run
- Astro Orbiter
- Dumbo the Flying Elephant
- Magic Carpets of Aladdin

Kid's Tip!

ROLLER COASTERS

If you don't know how much you like roller coasters, try The Barnstormer at the Magic Kingdom or Slinky Dog Dash at Hollywood Studios first. They are not scary at all, and they're over in a jiffy! If you like those, try one that is just a bit more exciting, like Seven Dwarfs Mine Train. If you still love it, you are ready for the most intense coasters of them all, Space Mountain, Expedition Everest and Rock 'n' Roller Coaster!

If you decide to try something even more exciting, see if you can sit in the front car of the coaster. This is the most fun because you don't have anything in front of you! (Sitting in front is also a smoother experience. The cars in the rear of the coaster tend to bang you around!)

If you want to sit in front, just ask the Cast Member when you reach the ride. There is a special place to wait—just a little off to the side—and it usually only adds a couple minutes to your overall wait time!

Epcot

- Guardians of the Galaxy: Cosmic Rewind
- Mission: SPACE
- Remy's Ratatouille Adventure
- Test Track
- Soarin' Around the World

Hollywood Studios

- Alien Swirling Saucers
- Millenium Falcon: Smugglers Run
- Rock 'n' Roller Coaster
- Slinky Dog Dash
- Star Tours
- Toy Story Mania

Animal Kingdom

- Flight of Passage
- Expedition Everest
- DINOSAUR
- Triceratop Spin

Things that Fright & Things that Excite!

It can be hard to tell if something is real or fake. For instance, the mechanical animals in The Jungle Cruise look very real and can scare people. Even movies, especially the 3-D ones, can have stuff that pops out and spooks kids. Other creepy things you might see are animated monsters and villains.

There are only a few live animals in the parks, besides the ones at Animal Kingdom. It is rare that any of the wild animals will scare you, because they really can't get too close.

Even the animals at the petting farm in Animal Kingdom are soft and furry, rather than big and fierce. (They have cute goats and cows you can meet in person!)

Mostly, the animals are fun to see and only frighten kids who have not yet seen live animals like tigers and giraffes. Ask your parents to show you what they look like on the Internet and you will see how beautiful they are.

Disney parks do have some local live animals that like to hang out there.

Look for ducks, squirrels, rabbits, lizards and white ibis (these are the white birds that can get very "friendly" as they search for food). If you are bothered by any of them, you can usually gently shoo them away and they will leave you alone. Just remember not to feed them.

Robotic Machines. Probably the spookiest thing at Disney are the robotic creatures, called Audio-Animatronics. This is a big word that Walt Disney made up. It means that they combine the voices and sounds ("audio") with the moving machines ("animated electronics") to look real. (When the parks started, this was still brand-new technology that Disney developed!)

Depending on the ride, you may see wild animals, bears, dinosaurs, insects and even spiders. If these get too scary, just remember that nothing can actually get to you. It is all make believe! They are simply machines operated by computers.

None of the scary creatures are real. You'll even laugh when you see Donald Duck's rear end in Philharmagic!

Films. Disney has the greatest film technology ever! The 4-D effects include creatures, like insects and spiders, scents and even mist. If these get too scary, you can just take off your special 3-D glasses or look away.

Themes. Some rides are scary just because of their themes. The Haunted Mansion sounds scary, doesn't it? The special effects that create the ghosts look very real!

Even the Tower of Terror sounds terrifying! But none of these rides are meant to be anything more than a lot of fun. You soon discover the pretend ghosts are just playing around and singing and want you to join in their fun!

Noises. There are instances of loud simulated gunfights, cannons or commotion that can be frightening. Remember these noises are just that - sounds! What you hear isn't actually happening, so enjoy the moment knowing that you're safe!

Live-action Performances and Scary Characters. Some characters can be scary. For example, Darth Vader is a bad guy ("villain") and he is very big. Another big character is Chewbacca. Even Goofy frightens some kids. He is one of the tallest guys in Disney World! Maleficent looks big and scary, but she doesn't hurt a fly. These Characters are all part of the Disney magic - they're fun to enjoy… even if they might not be smiling.

Here are a few things to look for on Disney attractions. You might be fearless and have a fun time on everything, but some kids like to know what to expect.

Motion

High speed

Fast spinning

Fast take off and inverted loops (on a rollercoaster — especially Rock 'N' Roller Coaster!)

Drops from tall heights (especially Tower of Terror, Tiana's Bayou Adventure, Expedition Everest)

Environment and Special Effects

Dark tunnels

Strobes and Laser effects

Loud noises, including some screaming

Simulated fights, including gunfights

Dark rooms, tunnels, open space

Small or confined areas

Famous Photography Faces! Disney takes a picture of you on lots of their rides. These photographs are usually taken at the point when you are the most excited!

This might be at the very beginning, like on Rock 'n' Roller Coaster, or closer to the end, like on Tiana's Bayou Adventure.

Stunts. All dangerous stunts are performed far away from the audience. You may see simulated (that means made to look real) disasters, explosions, smoke and flames - all of which are make-believe using special effects. Instead of getting frightened, try to figure out how Disney makes it all happen.

Getting Around: Walt Disney World Transportation

Introduction to the Magic Kingdom

Monorail

The monorail provides a fast method of getting around Disney World. Disney's monorail takes you here and there on a loop from the parking lot to the Magic Kingdom, passing by (and even through!) resorts along the way! A separate track travels all the way from the Magic Kingdom to Epcot.

Kid's Trivia!

Mono means "one" and, unlike most trains that have two tracks, this one runs on a single track. Walt got the idea for this revolutionary transit system at the 1962 Seattle World's Fair.

There are 12 monorail trains. Each one is identified by a colored stripe along the side. The 12 colors are:

1	Red
2	Coral
3	Orange
4	Gold
5	Yellow
6	Teal
7	Lime
8	Green
9	Blue
10	Silver
11	Black
12	Peach

Occasionally, one of the monorails is given a temporary "wrap" around its body, or it could be decorated with pictures to promote a recent movie release.

Want to learn a bit of Spanish? Ride the monorail!

You'll hear this phrase broadcast on a public address (PA) system upon boarding:

"Please stand clear of the doors" (English).

"Por favor manténganse alejado de las puertas" (Spanish).

This is one of the most well-known phrases within Walt Disney World; it was recorded by Jack Wagner, who is known as "the Voice of Disneyland."

Disney Buses

Disney Buses are the most popular way to get around. Buses take you from your Disney Resort to each of the four main Theme Parks, two Water Parks and Disney Springs. Buses even run from one park to another to help you save time.

Water Transportation

Water taxis (river boats) are known as *Friendship boats*. They're a fun way to get from *Point A* to *Point B*. For instance, you can catch a water taxi from either Port Orleans Resorts, Old Key West or Saratoga Springs and enjoy a boat ride to Disney Springs. It's free! Water Taxis are also available from some other resorts to Disney's Theme Parks.

Minnie Vans (Costs Money)

Do you and your family need to get somewhere quickly? For a small fee, an adult can arrange a Minnie Van to take you where you need to be! Minnie Vans are Disney's very own taxi-like service. They get the fun name because they're decorated with Minnie Mouse's famous spots. Just tell your parents to download the Lyft app and order a ride!

Disney Skyliner

If you're not in a hurry, you can try the fun Skyliner (sky tram) system. The Disney Skyliner takes you soaring through the air. Travel from Disney's Art of Animation, Pop Century, Caribbean Beach and Riviera Resorts to Disney's Hollywood Studios or the International Gateway at Epcot.

Kid's Tip!

Younger kids want to visit the Magic Kingdom over any other park. It has the most rides and was all made just for kids to enjoy with their entire family!

Kid's Tip!

Ask for some pixie dust at the Harmony Barber Shop. They'll give you a fresh sprinkling of it over your head!

Let's go to Magic Kingdom!

Introduction to the Magic Kingdom

The Magic Kingdom has the most to do and is the most fun for younger kids!

More!
More rides!
More shows!
More parades!

You don't have to be a kid to love the Magic Kingdom. Your parents and grandparents will love all it has to offer, too. It's full of enchantment! It's where you find thrilling rides, amazing entertainment, spectacular parades and magical nighttime fireworks shows.

Throughout the entire park, there are more than 30 attractions - almost twice as many as any other park! In the table at the end of this section, we list the top attractions you are going to want to consider for your family's agenda.

Opening Ceremony

Arrive at the park first thing in the morning to catch its Opening Ceremony where Mickey Mouse and all his friends greet their guests with a fabulous show at Cinderella Castle.

Cinderella Castle is located "smack dab-in-the-middle" of the Magic Kingdom.

Six Lands of the Magic Kingdom

The Castle is surrounded by six very different, themed areas, called *lands*. Each land is special in its own way and designed to transport you to a different time or place:

1. Visit Colonial America in Liberty Square.
2. See the 19th century Wild West in Frontierland.
3. Experience turn-of-the-century Americana in Main Street, U.S.A.
4. Go way back in time to medieval Europe in Fantasyland.
5. Have a timeless adventure through the Adventureland jungles.
6. Tomorrowland lets you travel at warp speed on a spaceship far into the future.

Liberty Square Highlights

Fun and History! Have a ball in the spooky Haunted Mansion, or learn about America's history in the Hall of Presidents.

Frontierland Highlights

Explore the new frontier: Big Thunder Mountain Railroad, Tiana's Bayou Adventure, and Tom Sawyer Island are each rootin'-tootin' fun!

Main Street U.S.A Highlights

Old-fashioned, small town fun is what this tribute to Walt's childhood is all about. Visit souvenir shops, a real train station (to travel on a steam locomotive around the park), an actual barber shop (Get your hair cut there!) and a fire station. You can even meet lots of great characters (especially Magician Mickey

Fantasyland
Liberty Square
Frontierland
Adventureland

MAGIC
Kingdom
Tomorrowland
Main St., U.S.A.

and Tinker Bell!). Don't miss the Evening Flag Retreat, a special ceremony that salutes America.

Tomorrowland Highlights

Futuristic rides zip you through the galaxy. Kids especially enjoy Buzz Lightyear's Space Ranger Spin and Space Mountain (Mega Thrill!).

Kids, Look up!

Hunt for weathervanes as you walk around the park. Look for the following ones:

- Rooster
- Moose
- Elf-like Troll with a Long Nose
- Crocodile

Do you spot others?

Adventureland Highlights

Visit the great unknown on Pirates of the Caribbean, Jungle Cruise and Enchanted Tiki Room.

Adventureland is the most exotic place you can imagine, just like Hawaii or the South Pacific.

Fantasyland Highlights

Story books come to life as you experience Peter Pan's Flight, Dumbo the Flying Elephant, Seven Dwarfs Mine Train (Most Popular Ride!), Little Mermaid, Enchanted Tales with Belle, and Be Our Guest Restaurant.

Fantasyland, set in old Europe, is the most classic and popular land. It's the place most people think of when imagining a trip to Disney World.

In this land, you become part of the story and get to live the whimsical world of Disney fairy tales.

Main Street, U.S.A.

This is a small, turn-of-the-century American town, set around the year 1900. In fact, Walt Disney designed Main Street to look a lot like Marceline, Missouri, the town where he grew up. Be sure to notice the street lights - they look like old-fashioned lamp posts!

In most early towns, the City Hall would be located within a couple of blocks of the Fire Department. Haberdasheries (That's a fancy name for a men's clothing store, but they also sell women and kids clothing at the Magic Kingdom's stores!), food service and other neighborhood businesses would be found close together. At the Magic Kingdom, the movie theater and restaurants are located across from city offices. There is also a real, working Barber Shop to get your hair cut and styled.

Main Street, U.S.A. is a great place to shop. You can find clothes, toys, balloons, souvenirs and candy! If you need a new embroidered hat (stitched with your name), there are many options at the shop called *The Chapeau*. (Pronounced "shap-oh" - this is the word for "hat" in the French language.)

Meals and Treats. Main Street is also the place to fill bellies with a hot meal and drool over sweet treats: hot cocoa, ice cream, chocolate and candies galore!

Kid's Trivia!

Roy Disney was a U.S. military veteran. He served in the U.S. Navy from 1917 to 1919.

Walt wanted to join, but he was too young to enlist during World War I and too old during World War II!

He found other ways to show his pride in America, including volunteering for the Red Cross Ambulance Corps and drawing patriotic cartoons for soldiers and civilians to enjoy.

Flag Lowering Ceremony. The Disney brothers were great *patriots* (meaning they loved and respected their home country, the United States of America). They wanted to show proper respect to their country and its military members at the American Disney parks.

Most towns have a city hall where the U.S. flag is raised at the beginning of the day. At Walt Disney, only Cast Members are at work early in the morning when the flag is raised each sunrise.

Each evening, the flag is lowered during a Flag Retreat (flag lowering) ceremony. During the ceremony, there is a proper showing of respect to United States active military and veterans. (Veterans are people who served in the military.) During this performance, Walt Disney's Main Street Band plays patriotic music, including the American National Anthem, *The Star Spangled Banner.*

Every day, flag lowering ceremonies happen across the nation, especially where the United States has its military stationed. Every military base lowers the flag (near dusk) while playing the National Anthem. (This song is actually broadcast from all the overhead public announcement systems on military bases. Anyone walking – or driving! – has to stop what they are doing to show respect.)

Please Show Proper Respect. If you see the flag being lowered, or hear the National Anthem, the proper way to act is to **stop moving and talking**. If you are American, face the flag and put your right hand over your heart until the anthem stops. During the song, the flag is lowered, folded and taken away. (If you are wearing a hat, you may salute the flag instead, which is how most former-military members show respect.) If you are not American, simply stand quietly until the ceremony is over.

Kid's Fun! Free candy samples are sometimes available at the Main Street Confectionary candy shop. Look at the cotton candy booth to see if a special password is posted to get your sweet treat!

Transportation around Town. A long time ago, before cars were invented, horse-drawn trolleys (as shown on this book cover!) were used to help people get around town. If you show up early in the day, you can see real horses and even hop aboard the omnibus for a trip down Main Street. (You will learn more about these forms of transportation in a bit.)

Meet Characters. There are several places in Main Street, and throughout the rest of the park, to meet your favorite characters.

Claim your parade or show viewing spot! Go early to get the best viewing locations on Main Street to watch a parade or street performance!

Walt Disney World Railroad. There is only one ride attraction in Main Street, a real locomotive train! You can board the train and journey around the entire park. Don't forget that Walt Disney loved trains. Look around the station for tributes to him.

Window Designs. At the front of each shop are classic window decorations. This was common to downtown businesses so people walking by the store could see what services or products the business owner (called a "proprietor") sold.

Business from Home. Look up to the second floor windows. Many years ago, downtown businesses often had an upstairs apartment where the business owner and his family lived. When the business owner was not busy, he would spend his time upstairs with his family. When he got busy, his wife and older kids could help run the shop.

Second Floor Windows. Second floor windows are really special on Main Street. The names of people written on them are real. Many are Disney Legends who helped build the parks!

Shopkeepers often owned their own business and sometimes lived above their shop, on the second floor. (Otherwise, the second floor might be used for storage or offices.)

Cinderella Castle. Cinderella Castle towers above everything down at the end of the Main Street. When you reach the end of the road, you enter what is called forecourt plaza or *The Hub*. This is a great central meeting place if your family decides to split up.

Why is it called The Hub? The center of a wheel is called a hub and is used here because the park is laid out like a wheel. The Hub lies at the center and each "spoke" represents a path that leads to one of the six different lands. The "wheel" is represented by the train and pathway that goes all around the park.

You can either stroll around the park in a circular path, or choose to make your way back to Cinderella Castle to easily take a new path to discover each land.

Historical Note: In old American towns, spires from the town church hovered high overhead, owing to personal beliefs that sustained the homesteaders. Citizens of Europe more commonly saw castle towers, which represented government and safety.

Church Bells Toll. It was common for cities to respect the end of the "work day" and ring their bells precisely at 5 pm. Even if the church was not near the center of downtown, it could still be seen (and heard) from a short distance away. At Disney World, a somber civil ceremony takes place each day to mark the end of the day.

Magic Kingdom Attractions

Main Street, U.S.A.

Walt Disney World Railroad

Walt Disney loved trains growing up. Walt and Roy had an uncle who was a train conductor. Their uncle would blow his horn every time he passed through town, letting both of the boys know they were being thought about from far off in the distance.

Train Backstory. Did you know that when Walt grew up and could finally afford it, he had a real miniature train set up in the backyard of his home? It was big

Disney Animated Movies

T	O	N	A	A	M	R	R	C	E	L	L	A	O
O	I	A	I	E	B	N	D	N	R	O	S	P	C
I	H	L	K	O	B	A	N	I	S	R	R	E	I
A	C	A	O	D	R	L	E	S	E	O	A	T	N
N	C	D	O	I	O	U	I	R	L	B	C	E	D
S	O	D	B	N	T	M	B	E	U	I	A	R	E
D	N	I	E	O	H	T	M	T	C	N	C	P	R
E	I	N	L	S	E	A	A	S	R	H	F	A	E
L	P	T	G	A	R	R	B	N	E	O	O	N	L
G	M	L	N	U	B	Z	I	O	H	O	A	E	L
N	O	O	U	R	E	A	T	M	E	D	A	S	A
A	A	B	J	U	A	N	O	B	M	U	D	M	A
T	A	D	C	L	R	A	I	S	A	T	N	A	F
L	U	B	T	S	W	A	L	L	E	R	B	L	E

WALL-E
PETER PAN
TARZAN
BAMBI
BROTHER BEAR
ROBIN HOOD
CARS
JUNGLE BOOK
PINOCCHIO
TANGLED
BOLT
MULAN
MONSTERS INC
CINDERELLA
ALADDIN
HERCULES
DUMBO
FANTASIA
DINOSAUR

enough for his guests to ride aboard. (Walt was the locomotive engineer!)

Walt Disney World Railroad. Walt's love of trains meant he absolutely had to have trains in his parks. Train tracks circle the entire park for families to enjoy. It is a fun way to get around in style, and it gives you a break when your feet get sore or your legs get tired.

Carolwood Pacific Railroad was the name Walt gave to the 1/8th scale steam train and railroad he operated. (Look for pictures of him with his train near the stroller rental counter as you enter the park.)

Train Stations. Besides the station at Main Street, U.S.A., there are two other stations, one at Frontierland and the other at Fantasyland. You can get on and off at these other stations, so it's a great way to travel!

Kid's Review! We really love the 20-minute journey all the way around the park. During the trip there are a few things to see, including a small outpost, a Native American Village and some "wildlife!"

Locomotives. All four of the steam-powered train engines are about 100 years old! The four locomotives are named the Walter E. Disney, the Roy O. Disney, the Lilly Belle and the Roger E. Broggie. (Broggie was an Imagineer who also really loved trains!)

Kid's Tip!

If you sit in the back row of the very last train car, the Conductor just might ask you to yell "All Aboard!" into the microphone!

Kid's Tip!

During your journey, the conductor tells you fun facts about the park. It's fun and you stay in the shade, which is perfect when it gets hot outside!

Main Street Vehicles

If you visit the Magic Kingdom early in the day, you just might see one or more of the following classic vehicles.

- Horse-drawn street car, an old-fashioned trolley pulled by a horse
- Jitney, an early automobile with no roof
- Fire Engine, a replica of the earliest fire truck
- Omnibus, a gas-powered, open-air, two-story bus

Did you know? The earliest bus was enclosed and horse-drawn and is also called a horsebus. Omnibus has the Latin base "omni" that means "for all" so this means any type of vehicle used to transport multiple passengers. At Disney, the word omnibus means one that is engine-powered. The word "bus" is short for omnibus.

Not all of these vehicles are used every day. Stop by City Hall in Town Square to find out their schedule on the day you visit.

Grab a family member or friend and hop aboard a vehicle for a one-way trip up or down Main Street. The journey takes you between Town Square (at the front of the park) and the court in front of Cinderella Castle ("forecourt").

Kid's Tip!

When the horses need to take a break, you can see them as they relax in the Car Barn near the Emporium on Main Street.

Hidden Mickey Alert!

Check out the *Partners Statue*, a bronze statue of Walt Disney holding the hand of Mickey Mouse in the Castle Forecourt. Don't leave without a picture of this famous statue.

Town Square

Town Square Theater

All day long, you can meet Mickey or Tinker Bell within the Town Square Theater. If lines are short, ask your parents if you can meet both!

If you plan to meet Mickey Mouse, remember that he travels from park to park, so you can meet him on whatever day is most convenient. What's really fun is that he changes his clothes depending on which park it is. For instance, at the Magic Kindom, Mickey dresses as a Magician and might perform a trick or two for you!

Be sure to take your camera for family pictures - and a video recording of your meeting with Mickey, too!

Use a Lightning Lane reservation to meet Mickey if you want to skip the line. It tends to move slowly because of all the one-on-one time each guest gets with Mickey!

Adventureland

The best way to picture Adventureland in your mind is to think of remote jungles in Africa, Asia, South America and the South Pacific. Think exotic adventure, lush vegetation, totem poles, congo drums, tribal masks—a land filled with undiscovered mysteries!

Adventureland is divided into two main areas: the Arabian Village and the Caribbean Plaza. This is home to the awesome ride that inspired a blockbuster movie series, *Pirates of the Caribbean*. (That's right - the ride came before the movies!)

Hidden Mickey Alert!

Crossing the bridge from Main Street, U.S.A, look for a carving of Mickey's head in the tribal shields above the path.

Jungle Cruise

Take a water voyage aboard a riverboat through the jungles of Asia and Africa. Be sure to keep an eye out for zebras, giraffes, hippopotamuses, lions, headhunters and more!

The boating adventure gets crowded throughout the day. Try to get here early in the morning or late in the evening for shorter lines. If you ride it after the fireworks, the evening journey is creepier! You can usually get a Lightning Lane reservation for this ride to avoid long waits.

The *skipper* loves to tell corny jokes as he takes you on your boat ride. (The "skipper" is your boat captain and tour guide.) Try to remember as many jokes as you can. Which one is your favorite?

Hidden Mickey Alert!

Check out the rock behind the Bathing Elephants… Do you see it?

Pirates of the Caribbean

Pirates of the Caribbean may sound like a scary ride, but look a little deeper into the details and you realize it's clever and fun! The cool discoveries begin before you even get on the ride.

As you're standing in the queue, before you start the boat ride, look for two skeletons playing chess. A popular rumor says that the chess board is set up in a stalemate (no legal moves remain available for either player). This implies that the two pirates sat playing the game, unable to make a move, until both died.

Keep a lookout on your left after you start the ride. *Can you spot the spooky mermaid skeleton?*

Once you're on the ride, you float through a pirate-ghost mist where you may hear an ominous warning. For younger kids, this may be the scariest portion of the ride. Up ahead is a dark area, where your boat "slides" down into the bay—don't worry, this drop is easy compared to Tiana's Bayou Adventure. This small portion of the ride is like an indoor roller coaster when it drops, but it is more fun than frightening. The only kids who might be afraid of this are a really young brother or sister who is afraid of the dark. (If you are old enough to read this yourself, you are going to LOVE this ride!)

"To create a land that would make this dream reality," said Walt Disney, "we pictured ourselves far from civilization, in the remote jungles of Asia and Africa."

Excitement Factor! Pirates of the Caribbean is an exciting ride with many Audio-Animatronic characters.

Look for the big pirate ship in the middle of the bay. *Watch out!* You're in the middle of the action as the pirates attack a small seaside village with lots of cannon fire! Don't worry, though. They aren't actual cannons!

The special effects just make it seem like the balls are really firing at you when the shots "hit" in the water a few feet away.

Flashes of light and blasts of air from beneath the water give the illusion of cannon balls being fired at you, but missing and landing in the water.

Later on, look for pirates looting and pillaging a village. There's a really fun scene where a lady is chasing an invading pirate with her broomstick!

Throughout your Caribbean Adventure, you get to sing along with the ever-familiar, "Yo Ho, Yo Ho, a Pirate's Life for Me!"

Magic Kingdom Favorites

Across

2. Meet Magician ________ at his theater on on Main Street, U.S.A.

4. Big _______ is the "wildest ride in the West!"

6. There are 999 spooks in the ________ Mansion.

7. It's a Small ________ After All!

10. Captain Jack _________ stars in a pirate adventure.

Down

1. The Mad Hatter cordially invites you to take a spin at his ________ Party.

3. Fly high with Aladdin on a magic ________ in Adventureland.

5. Tom ________ had many adventures on an island in Frontierland.

8. What flying elephant takes you on a spin in Fantasyland?

9. Who owns this castle where you're invited to Be Our Guest?

*Answers on Page 213

Hidden Mickey Alert!

Look for the singing donkey. His ears cast a shadow of Mickey.

A SAD NOTE! Pirates of the Caribbean was the last attraction for which Walt Disney oversaw the construction (in Disneyland) before he passed away.

Did you know? The ride was around long before the movie series! The attraction has been a mainstay at the Magic Kingdom since it opened on December 15, 1973. The first of the movies, Pirates of the Caribbean: The Curse of the Black Pearl, didn't arrive at the theaters until 2003. How many years later is that?

The first movie took scenes right out of Disney's attraction! If you saw the movie, you are going to recognize many elements, such as the jail keeper's dog and pirate prisoners. Going full circle, Disney updated the ride after the movies became a huge hit. You now get to see Captain Jack Sparrow in odd places and situations throughout the attraction!

A Pirate's Adventure ~ Treasures of the Seven Seas

Ahoy mateys! Search for treasure in this walking adventure through Adventureland.

Just head to the old Cartography (map) Shop to sign up for one of four different treasure hunts. You even get a real treasure map to take home!

When you discover each checkpoint on your map, something special happens. At the end of your hunt, you get a surprise keepsake — all for free!

The best part is, as soon as you finish one adventure, you can sign up for another. It's so much fun, you'll want to do it over and over again!

The Magic Carpets of Aladdin

Fly high over Agrabah on a magic carpet ride! Aladdin may have gotten three wishes from his genie-in-the-lamp, but the rest of us get this awesome, fair-style ride that goes around in circles. It is a lot like the Dumbo the Flying Elephant ride in Fantasyland, except with spitting camels!

Kid's Tip!

Riders who sit in the front row get a lever that raises and lowers the carpet. If you lower it at the right time, water from a "spitting camel" splashes you — and whoever is sitting behind you — just a little bit!

This high-flying ride gives an excellent overhead view of Adventureland, which is dressed up to look like the desert village Agrabah, from the movie Aladdin.

Characters sometimes show up in this area to meet with kids and take pictures with them! Make sure to get their autographs!

Swiss Family Treehouse

The Swiss Family Robinson is the title of a book written in 1812 by author Johann Wyss. He based his fun writing on adventure tales he and his children made up. The book has stories about the Swiss family (from Switzerland) that survives a shipwreck and becomes stranded on a deserted island. The Robinson family then has to fend off pirates and experiences other zany adventures.

Walt Disney Productions (the name of Disney's film studio business) made the movie in 1960 based entirely on the book by Mr. Wyss.

Excitement Factor! You get to climb a real tree house high in the sky!

The tall treehouse at the Magic Kingdom closely resembles the original one used in the film. This is a walking (really a "stair-stepping") attraction, which means you get to explore the treehouse at your own pace!

Be prepared to move those legs—you go up and down 116 steps on different floors. But the climbing is worth it! There is an excellent view of the Magic Kingdom from up above. It's also a great place to see the fireworks at night. You can't get Lightning Lane reservations for the tree house, and you don't need them. There's almost never a wait to enter.

Guess what? The Swiss Family Treehouse isn't built on a tree at all—the body is built with a strong, solid-steel structure to fully support all those people climbing up and down.

The tree "roots" are made of concrete and steel bars that extend into the ground 42 feet. That is four-stories deep! The carving looks so real, you would never guess that it's not a real tree. Its 300,000 leaves are made of plastic and can withstand the winds and rain of Florida—these leaves never fall!

Kid's Trivia!

Can you guess where else in Walt Disney World there is a man-made tree that looks real? That's right, it's the Tree of Life in Animal Kingdom!

Kid's Trivia!

California's Disneyland has Tarzan's Treehouse, rather than the Swiss Family Treehouse in its Adventureland.

Walt Disney's Enchanted Tiki Room

Sing along with bird buddies José, Michael, Fritz and Pierre at this Audio-Animatronic show. These wisecracking birds love to tell funny jokes!

Guests have been singing "In the Tiki, Tiki, Tiki, Tiki, Tiki Room" for about 50 years, and the attraction exists at Disneyland, too!

In the Tiki Room, birds aren't the only ones that sing. The flowers sing too and the carved masks hanging in the wall actually move! The show takes place all around you. The loud thunderstorm at the end can spook some young kids - but remember, it's just pretend!

Hidden Mickey Alert!

Look at the bird perches to spy a couple of Hidden Mickeys.

Frontierland

Have a real Wild West adventure! This could have been the most unlawful place in all the Magic Kingdom, but a new sheriff named Woody is in town! Now it's just fun to explore Disney's Old West ghost town.

Kid's Trivia!

"Ghost town" doesn't mean a place is haunted. This term refers to a town from which everybody has moved away and left it abandoned. Lots of Old West towns became ghost towns during the gold rush of the 1800s. People moved in to mine the area, then left as soon as the gold ran out!

The Three Mountains

There may not be a lot of rides in Frontierland, but they are some of the ones that give us the best thrills. Two of the three "Disney mountains" are right next to each other! You can travel on a runaway train through a haunted gold mine and get soggy wet on the best flume ride in the world within a few steps of each other!

Disney lovers know about the three "mountains" in Magic Kingdom: Space Mountain, Tiana's Bayou Adventure (formerly Splash Mountain) and Big Thunder Mountain Railroad. These are all wild rides and not for the faint of heart! Lots of people say Seven Dwarfs Mine Train actually means there are *four mountains* in the park, even though the word "mountain" isn't in the title.

Do you know where the final, and fifth Disney World mountain is? It's the wildest Disney ride of all: Expedition Everest in Animal Kingdom!

Kid's Trivia!

As the West was won (meaning that it was explored and people built their homes and businesses), many small wilderness frontier towns were established. These towns had to be close enough in distance where horses could easily travel from one to the other in a single day. This usually meant that they were no more than about 20 miles apart. They sprung up everywhere, but none of these towns were ever as fun as the one at Disney World.

Good vittles (this means food!) can be found at Pecos Bill Tall Tale Inn and Cafe. It has some of the best Southwest and Mexican eats anywhere. As a bonus, you can usually find fun, frontier games to play just outside the restaurant, on your way to Adventureland.

The Frontierland Shootin' Arcade is a laser-rifle firing range that lets you polish your shooting skills using lever-action long guns. There are dozens of targets in the nighttime scene of a western village.

(There used to be a charge to play this fun game, but it's now free!)

Kid's Trivia!

What is a flume? In the old days, before big trucks were available to haul timber (trees), woodsmen used to move logs down the mountain using water flumes along rivers and lakes. This is what inspired today's theme park log ride rides.

Kid's Trivia!

Note the building addresses in Frontierland. These numbers represent the year that each building style was common in the real West!

Tom Sawyer Island

Explore a real island and meet other kids! Most of us love taking a raft across the small river to the island where Tom Sawyer had a lot of fun when he was young. (He is the main character in the *The Adventures of Tom Sawyer* book, written by Mark Twain. See page 113 for more details about this author - he was a big deal!)

Wandering wonderment! Wander down the paths and up the hills, while having fun running across a real rope bridge and barrel bridge! After that, visit the windmill building and explore a real fort.

Imagine hiding out in each of the island's caves. Look for the secret exit that leads through a dark and narrow cave. (Caves can be a little scary, but not when you find an older buddy to go through with you!)

An Audio-Animatronic blacksmith lets you watch his progress as he creates horse-shoes and builds other metal contraptions.

Tom Sawyer Island is a pretty big area with a lot of paths to run down. Calm, tame and quieter than other places at the Magic Kingdom, it also has nicely shaded areas where your parents will appreciate relaxing while you run wild!

Tom Sawyer Island is not open past dusk (when the sun goes down), so get there early in the day.

Kid's Tip!

If your parents grumble about being tired, but you have lots of energy, head to Tom Sawyer Island. You can play all you want while they relax!

Tiana's Bayou Adventure (Opening in 2024)

You're going to love this ride. It is almost everyone's favorite for thrills! Follow the exploits of Tiana and her swamp friends as they plan a huge party. All of your favorites are there from Disney's film, *The Princess and the Frog*.

Near the end of your search, you drop with him down a tall waterfall. It's impossible to guarantee you'll stay dry. Expect to get a little wet, and there is a chance you might get drenched!!!

There are three small hill drops inside the ride. One last, slow uphill trip takes you to the final big splashdown to the bottom of the mountain. Remember to smile, because your picture is taken just as the log starts to drop! Try to keep your eyes open for the picture before you squeeze them closed for the landing!

Minimum Height Required:
40" tall (3 feet, 4 inches)

Kid's Tip!

The front, right side tends to get you the wettest, but the first rows always get drenched - try the left seat, back row if you want to stay slightly drier OR request to sit in the front to get soaked!

Hidden Mickey Alert!

In the final scene after the waterfall plunge, look for a sleeping Mickey high in the clouds.

Big Thunder Mountain Railroad

Not all kids love roller coasters, but those who do think this one is excellent! It is called, "The Wildest Ride in the Wilderness!"

The scene is set in an old, deserted gold mining town. Cursed runaway mine trains take you up and over the mountain top and through the town at breakneck speeds! Notice all the awesome scenery that looks just like a real working gold mine did over a hundred years ago! Keep an eye out for chickens, donkeys, goats and other animals. Did you see the poor, old man soaking in his outdoor bathtub?

Kid's Tip!

Big Thunder feels different at night than it does during the day. Try to go on it early and then right before you go home, after dark.

HELPFUL HINT: This tame ride is a good test to see what to expect on even bigger roller coasters! If you are at all nervous, go on Big Thunder Mountain Railroad before you try Space Mountain.

There are not too many abrupt dips on Big Thunder Mountain Railroad. If you're going up a large hill, expect you'll be riding back down! There are a few fun rolling hills and fast turns!

Sharp turns may scare some kids, especially if they get squished from a bigger kid or adult sitting next to them! The lap bar only drops down to the highest lap. For this reason, try to sit with another kid, or you might feel yourself fly around a little bit too much. It can be thrilling and a little scary if you feel like you might fall out, but you won't!

Minimum Height Required:
40" tall (3 feet, 4 inches)

Hidden Mickey Alert!

When you exit the ride, look for a prickly cactus with a familiar shape.

Frontierland Shootin' Arcade

Howdy pardner! Take aim and test your frontier shooting skills with a replica .54-caliber Hawkins buffalo rifle.

Special surprises await when you and other sharp-shooting bandits hit your targets in this Wild West-themed shooting arcade. It's so much fun!

Country Bear Jamboree

Who doesn't love a hoedown?! The Country Bear Jamboree is a goofy and fun country music show made especially for younger kids (but older kids, parents and grandparents enjoy it too)!

The stars of the show tell funny jokes while singing and playing lively music. More than a dozen (12) furry bears sing and play instruments like guitars, drums and banjos.

Big Al is a crowd favorite. The silly big bear never really learned to sing!

The mounted animal heads on the wall—Melvin the moose, Buff the buffalo and Max the deer—join in the merriment. The audience is encouraged to sing and clap along. You can even stomp your feet if you want to!

Even if you're not really into the music, it's a great place to spend a few minutes to rest when you are feeling hot. The show is held inside a really cool building!

Kid's Review! Even if you don't like country music, you will still laugh at some of the silly jokes.

Liberty Square

America had a time called the Colonial Period, when our country was brand new. During those early days, big cities like Philadelphia added grand designs for important buildings. Big columns and really tall ceilings were common in a lot of these buildings. You see this type of *architecture* all over Liberty Square, because it is supposed to be set in the Colonial days.

Liberty Square is the smallest Magic Kingdom land. It connects Frontierland and Fantasyland. The land is mostly about interesting tidbits from history, but it's definitely worth a visit even for non-history buffs. That's because one of the best and most thrilling attractions is there: *The Haunted Mansion*.

KID'S TRIVIA!

Philadelphia was especially important to America, because the Declaration of Independence was adopted by Congress in this city on July 4, 1776. This document led to the War for Independence, also known as the Revolutionary War. It is because of this fight for freedom from British colonial rule that we celebrate Independence Day on July 4th every year.

KID'S TRIVIA!

What's one thing you won't find in Liberty Square? Restrooms! That's right—in keeping with realism for "the times" in which this land is set, Disney Imagineers chose not to include actual restrooms (so, be sure to take your restroom break before entering)! Imagineers even went the extra mile and designed a brown pathway that runs through the center of the street. This represents sewage that would have been running through the town's sidewalks in the 1700s. *Yuck!*

Paul Revere's Midnight Ride. While touring Liberty Square, keep an eye out for two lanterns in a window. These represent the *Midnight Ride of Paul Revere*. He needed to warn colonials exactly how the British invaders were arriving, so they devised a special signal, "One if by land, two if by sea."

Can you guess how the British arrived? The Imagineers make sure you learn your United States history!

Check out the window near the lanterns—do you see a musket? This means a Minute Man lived here who was ready to fight for the new country. (Minute Man means a militia member who was ready in a minute, if needed.)

Most of these fighters were untrained farmers who believed the United States should be a free country. They were fierce and fought hard to win the battle for freedom from the King of England!

Liberty Belle Riverboat

Why not try a very rare experience, like floating around the river on a real sternwheel paddle boat, just like those that traveled the mighty Mississippi River? (The stern is the back of the boat, which is where the waterwheel is located.)

The Liberty Belle is an authentic replica of an old paddle wheel riverboat. Chill out on a 15- to 20-minute river cruise around the Rivers of America waterway (the river that circles Tom Sawyer Island).

Look for her boarding station at the covered dock, attached to the landing building. It is next door to the Haunted Mansion.

Claim a spot up front if you want to take a lot of great pictures, or stand in the back where you can see along both sides of the boat. Not only is the trip excellent, there are cool sights that can only be seen by taking this journey.

Although the Liberty Belle is very large—she holds up to 450 guests!—there are not a lot of seats, so you might have to stand when it's busy.

The Haunted Mansion

The Haunted Mansion is a spooky (but not too scary) haunted house that claims to be "home to 999 ghosts." (They are always looking for one more!) Walt Disney himself wanted the attraction to be family-friendly, so there are lots of silly scenes along with mildly scary stuff, including many ghouls.

An interactive line (queue) area makes waiting for the ride a lot of fun. There are plenty of entertaining props to touch and discover along the way!

Be sure to read the headstones while waiting in line—they have funny sayings on them like "Here lies good old Fred. A great big rock fell on his head." Look for the tombstone with a face. It has eyes, a nose and a mouth that move!

Kid's Tip!

Read the five tombstones at the beginning of the queue carefully. The messages are actually riddles. Solve each riddle to find out how each person died and who killed whom!

You begin your haunted adventure in the funeral parlor. The whole group gets "locked" in the creepy room before realizing there are *no windows*, *no doors* and *no way to escape*! Suddenly, the room starts to stretch downward… shortly before becoming pitch black. (Don't worry, it's over in just a few seconds.)

Once you escape the parlor (whew!), board a *Doom Buggy* for a slow journey through the house, up to the attic and then outside and down to the graveyard.

As you travel inside the Haunted Mansion, your Doom Buggy takes you past a creepy book case full of ghost stories, an organ that plays by itself (look at the shadow on the floor!) and glowing footsteps. There are so many fun and mildly spooky sights, you may have to go again to spot them all!

Be on the lookout for freaky door knockers and a floating tea pot pouring tea for a ghost tea party. If you need a laugh, check out the dancing ghosts–try to spot the funny sleeping one under the table in the grand ballroom!

Famous hitchhiking ghosts catch up to you at the end of the ride. This is one of the highlights. Just wait until you see what fun tricks they have in store for you!

Attraction Reaction! Scary... The ghost theme can scare kids (and some adults) - but only until they realize it's all good fun! The momentary darkness in the parlor room mentioned above makes some kids scream a little. Hold onto someone's hand and it won't be nearly as scary. And remember, it's all special effects and just meant to be a lot of silliness and laughs!

Kid's Tip!

There may be 999 happy haunts within the Mansion, but only 109 of them are Disney-created Audio-Animatronics! The rest are created with other types of special effects.

Hidden Mickey Alert!

In one of the last rooms of the mansion (before heading "outside" to the graveyard), look for a classic, three-circle Mickey.

Hall of Presidents

The Hall of Presidents, "A Celebration of Liberty's Leaders," is a multimedia show featuring Audio-Animatronics and pictures. They tell the origins and development of the United States government. It's an awesome stage show with all the (Audio-Animatronics) Presidents of the U.S. looking dignified!

When walking into the building, notice the entry room is a rotunda with a dome in the ceiling that lets light in. The sunlight shines down on the Presidential Seal, which you can see located in the center of the room.

Happy Haunts!

People report seeing real ghosts in Walt Disney World every year. These aren't scary spooks, though. Even the ghosts are having a great time in the parks!

Here are just a few of the legends. You can decide if you believe them or if they're just a bunch of funny, made-up stories.

Spaceship Earth in Epcot has a pair of kids, a boy and girl, playing in front of the attraction entrance. Some people even claim to see them on the ride!

Another Epcot attraction, *Impressions de France*, has a spook who haunts the theater. He suddenly disappears when Cast Members try to escort him out!

Do you think the *Twilight Zone Tower of Terror* is the spookiest ride in Walt Disney World? We agree—and so does the ghost who lives there! Look on Platform D if possible, around the last ride of the evening. You might see a ghostly bellhop creating some mischief!

Haunted Mansion in Magic Kingdom is haunted by 999 ghosts that we already know about, but there may be two more spirits who have made this attraction their home. An older gentleman with a cane seems to really love riding the Doom Buggies late at night. Legend says he was an airplane pilot who crashed into (what is now) Bay Lake back in the 1940s—before Walt Disney World was built!

It's the little boy ghost that most kids want to meet, though. He enjoys his favorite ride all the way into the afterlife. You might see him peek around a Doom Buggy to smile at you!

Possibly the best-known spirit in the Magic Kingdom is George. He was helping to build the *Pirates of the Caribbean* attraction when he met his untimely demise. To this day, Cast Members greet George with a friendly "Good Morning" and "Good Night" each day over the intercom. If they forget, George is thought to cause the ride to break down! (Beware: don't say you don't believe in George while riding. Many guests claim he stops the ride, forcing them to leave early!)

Of all the spirits in Walt Disney World, none is as beloved as a man who roams Main Street, U.S.A. Still standing vigil over his family's creation is the one-and-only Roy Disney, Walt's brother. He passed away less than three months after the Magic Kingdom opened, but guests still say they see him walking the street and smiling at all the happy visitors!

What do you believe?

Kid's Trivia!

The first Audio-Animatronic character that was ever created was Abraham Lincoln. You can see the original one that was used in the 1964 New York's World Fair at the *Walt Disney Presents* attraction in Hollywood Studios.

If you like history, take a look around the room. There are cool artifacts, paintings and even authentic, antique furniture for you to see!

The performance is located inside a fancy, 700-seat theater with a multi-screen projection system. The attraction is updated every four to eight years when a new president is elected (depending on whether or not the sitting president gets re-elected). Do you recognize our current president?

Did You Know? The Hall of Presidents is the only other place the Presidential Seal of the United States can be seen, other than at the White House in Washington, DC. Disney folks convinced Congress to allow them to display it. Now that's determination!

The presidents and other figures are very realistic! They actually shift around and even whisper to one another! In fact, Imagineers wanted the Presidents to be as life-like as possible, so Franklin D. Roosevelt is wearing leg braces underneath his pant legs! (Did you know he was disabled and had to use a wheelchair?)

That's right - even though no one ever sees them - the Imagineers wanted to go the extra mile to be realistic.

Only a few of the founding fathers, including George Washington and Abraham Lincoln, have speaking roles. The current President also speaks to us!

Kid's Trivia!

Do you know the first words of the Declaration of Independence?

"We hold these truths to be self-evident, that all men are created equal, that they are endowed by their Creator with certain unalienable Rights, that among these are Life, Liberty and the pursuit of Happiness."

Fantasyland

This is where the magic begins, just behind Cinderella Castle! Some people call it "Storybook Central." Many Disney movies are represented here, including some of the best fairytales, such as Cinderella, Peter Pan, Pinocchio, Winnie the Pooh, Snow White and the Seven Dwarfs, and many others!

Fantasyland is the best land for kids!

All kids and even adults love visiting here. Because it's such a popular land, it becomes busy pretty early in the morning and many of the attractions quickly get long lines.

Kid's Tip!

The best time to visit Fantasyland is first thing in the morning or during the nighttime shows and fireworks (if you've already seen them!).

Prince Charming Regal Carrousel

This is an authentic fair ride that was built over 100 years ago (1917) and discovered in New Jersey by Disney folks. They bought it and completely rebuilt the ride, before moving it to its location behind Cinderella Castle.

Note: Disney spells the word carousel in the title using an additional "r." This is an old-fashioned way to spell the word.

Each hand-carved horse on the carousel is completely unique. Be sure to look up and notice the hand-painted scenes from Cinderella on the ceiling!

The carousel rotates to the best Disney soundtrack with tunes like "*Be Our Guest*" and "*When You Wish Upon a Star.*"

Mad Tea Party

The Mad Tea Party is a spinning teacup ride inspired by the Unbirthday Party scene in Disney's Alice in Wonderland. You get to ride in teacups, which rotate as they move around a huge, spinning platform. Each individual cup spins faster if you turn a big steering wheel in your lap.

Whirl 'round and 'round at a dizzying pace for about one and a half (1½) minutes (90 seconds). Look towards the center of the ride to see the mouse peek out from his giant teacup!

This fun ride can make some kids dizzy. Whatever you do, don't go on this ride shortly after eating!

Kid's Tip!

If you start feeling sick on the ride, *focus on something on the horizon* (off in the distance) and *stop spinning the wheel*.

The Barnstormer

Goofy's wild roller coaster is found in Storybook Circus. It contains twists and turns like an acrobatic airplane flight that soars into the sky and swoops down low. It's a coaster meant especially for children, so the small cars are best for kids - but parents can certainly join in, too!

Be sure to hang on tight! Even older kids love the speed!

The ride starts out slow but picks up a lot of speed. It is fast and thrilling, but ends quickly as it's only 30 seconds long; that's just a half minute! Because this is a really short ride, it's great for beginners to find out if they like roller coasters!

Minimum Height Required:
35" tall (2 feet, 11 inches)

Kid's Trivia!

Dumbo the Flying Elephant is one of the original Walt Disney World attractions, meaning it was there back when the park opened in 1971 (even though it looks a little different now). Do you know all the original attractions that are still there?

- Country Bear Jamboree
- Dumbo the Flying Elephant
- Frontierland Shootin' Arcade (called Frontier Shooting Gallery then)
- Hall of Presidents
- Haunted Mansion
- it's a small world!
- Jungle Cruise
- Mad Tea Party
- Main Street Vehicles
- Prince Charming Regal Carrousel (called Cinderella's Golden Carrousel then)
- Swiss Family Treehouse
- Tom Sawyer Island (although guests couldn't visit until 1973)
- Tomorrowland Speedway (called Grand Prix Raceway then)
- Walt Disney World Railroad
- Walt Disney's Enchanted Tiki Room (called Tropical Serenade then)

Dumbo the Flying Elephant

The line for Dumbo the Flying Elephant in Storybook Circus takes you into a circus tent. There's a full playground inside where you can run around and play while waiting to take your flight aboard an elephant.

This attraction is based on Dumbo, the Disney film about the flying elephant.

There are two separate Dumbo rides. If you notice, they actually spin in opposite directions.

Typically, the lines are short early in the day and after dark when a lot of younger children start going home. If there is a long line when you arrive, don't worry! That's just a great excuse to take some time to get out of the sun and play in the huge circus tent.

Cast Members give your parents a pager to keep your place in "line." Your folks get to sit down and rest a spell. If you are under 12 years old, you get lots of play time until it's your turn to ride.

Dumbo is a short, two-minute ride. When you are on board, look for the lever that lets you control the up and down movement as you rotate in a big circle.

Small kids (3-8) love Dumbo! If you have a younger brother or sister, put this on your list of rides to experience with them.

HINT: Get a Lightning Lane reservation if you don't want to spend time playing in the tent!

Casey Jr. Splash 'N' Soak Station

The Casey Jr. Splash 'N' Soak Station is a water play area with crazy camels, monkeys, giraffes and elephants who splash along with guests. There is a parked train with four different rail cars carrying circus characters.

Kids love to jump in puddles and run through the spraying circus animals! You can really get soaked—it's a great way to cool off in the hot sun!

Kid's Tip!

Ask your parents to take along a change of clothes or wear a swimsuit under your clothes! You can dry off in the nearby restrooms.

Peter Pan's Flight

Take off to Neverland with Wendy, Tinker Bell and Peter Pan! Peter Pan's Flight allows you to soar high into the nighttime skies of London in a flying pirate ship. Look for the tiny cars moving on the roads below. The ride is very smooth, as your fun flight takes off from the ground and soars high. (If you look closely, you can see that the track is actually up in the air - what the engineers call aerial).

Be on the lookout for Captain Hook and his dedicated sidekick, Mr. Smee. Also look for Tik Tok (the name of the crocodile that swallowed an alarm clock!) trying to catch the angry Captain Hook.

Peter Pan's Flight is amazing and fun; it's recommended for everybody!

HINT: Get a Lightning Lane reservation if you can. This ride often has a really long wait time. If you have to wait, though, the interactive queue is super cool!

Nearby is the regal Princess Fairytale Hall. This is where Cinderella and several of her princess friends greet guests all day long!

"it's a small world"

"it's a small world" is a timeless classic attraction, because it's been around since opening day of the Magic Kingdom. (It can also be found at Disneyland.) You'll enjoy this relaxing boat ride as you travel through countries across the globe! This attraction celebrates people and cultures from all over the world. We learn that we are more alike than not.

Kid's Tip!

This attraction was built long before Walt Disney World. With the help of artist Mary Blair, Imagineers created the ride for the 1964 New York World's Fair. It was so popular, they had to put it in Disneyland and then in the Magic Kingdom when it opened in 1971.

See boys and girls wearing traditional clothing from their countries. They sing the theme song, *It's a Small World After All*, a few times over, sometimes in their own language! These doll figurines are mechanical and, though not technically Audio-Animatronics, still super fun to watch!

Look for the Japanese boy flying his kite, the Scottish bagpipers and even Polynesian hula dancers. Can you spot the jungle animals? Try to find hippos, monkeys and giraffes.

As you reach the end of the ride, the words "Good Bye" are written in languages from all over the world.

Did you know? The theme song is sung in five different languages during the ride. Over 100 countries are represented in total!

Hidden Mickey Alert!

When you get into Africa, look at the vines.

The Many Adventures of Winnie the Pooh

The fun starts before you even get on this ride! Imagineers created a really fun interactive queue area with a kids-only journey through Pooh's house (a tree trunk). Play in a whimsical garden, steer the honey bees through a maze and wipe the Hunny Wall (*hunny* is how Pooh spells *honey*) to reveal hidden characters! (Be sure to wash your hands after touching the hunny walls!)

When you're ready to ride, hop aboard a giant Hunny Pot and travel through the pages of a Winnie the Pooh storybook. Adventure through the Hundred Acre Wood and help Pooh find his pots full of sticky, sweet honey.

Can you feel the howling winds and see the rustling and blowing leaves?

Here is how you say goodby in some of the foreign languages in *it's a small world*:

Country (Language)	
Tanzania (Swahili)	Kwa heri! ("kwaHEree") translates to goodbye with luck.
China (Chinese)	再见 ("zài jiàn") translates to see you again.
Denmark (Danish)	Farvel! ("fah-VEHL") translates to farewell.
France (French)	Au revoir! ("oh ruh-vwar") translates to until we meet again.
Hawaii (Hawaiian)	Aloha! ("əˈlōˌhä") translates to the breath of life and is how Hawaiians say both hello and goodbye.
Israel (Hebrew)	Shalom! ("shuh-lowm") translates to peace.
Italy (Italian)	Ciao! ("chau") means both hello and goodbye.
Japan (Japanese)	さようなら ("sahy-uh-nahr-uh") translates to if that's the way it is.
Mexico (Spanish)	Adios! ("ˌɑ.diˈoʊs") translates to I commend you.

These strong winds blow Piglet and Roo off their feet and threaten to blow Owl's treehouse away!

Have you always wanted to bounce with Tigger? Everyone gets in on the fun, because the whole Hunny Pot goes up and down!

Throughout the ride, many more of Pooh's friends appear. Try to spot them all!

Oh, Bother! When Pooh wakes to realize it was all a terrible dream, he sees that it is raining outside and his honey pots might get washed away in a flood. But the ride ends happily. Pooh gets his honey back and all his friends shout hooray!

HINT: Get a Lightning Lane reservation if this is important to get into your schedule!

Under the Sea – Journey of the Little Mermaid

Journey underwater with Ariel and become part of her world. Step aboard your own "clam-mobile"—a giant clamshell vehicle like the ones at The Seas with Nemo and Friends—and journey under the sea into Ariel's world!

This attraction contains a neat special effect that makes it seem like you're going under the sea, even though you don't actually get wet. There's a lot of amazing things to look at. You can sing favorite songs and help battle the giant sea witch, Ursula! Look for our favorite friends, including Flounder and Sebastian.

Kid's Tip!

Journey of the Little Mermaid usually has a pretty short wait later in the evening, so don't use a Lightning Lane reservation if there are other rides you want to do.

After the ride, visit Ariel's Grotto to meet The Little Mermaid face to face (and get an autograph and photo)!

Seven Dwarfs Mine Train

Seven Dwarfs Mine Train is a kid-friendly roller coaster with entertaining dips and curves. It's not super scary, just full of fun!

You'll see bazillions of sparkly diamonds and colorful gemstones in the mine where the seven dwarfs go off to work, singing "*Heigh-Ho, Heigh-Ho, It's Off to Work We Go!*"

What's unique about the ride is the special special train cars that sway side-to-side while going around turns. It is a fast ride up and down the mountainside, but tamer than Space Mountain, gentler than Big Thunder Mountain Railroad, and without big drops like Tiana's Bayou Adventure. It is surprising how smooth it is!

As the ride ends, be sure to check out the dwarfs' home on your right hand side where they are celebrating with Snow White — Who's that standing at the door with an apple?!

If the Barnstormer roller coaster thrills you, this coaster is even faster and a lot less jerky.

Minimum Height Required:
38" tall (3 feet, 2 inches)

Kid's Trivia!

Can you name all of the seven dwarfs?

1. Sleepy
2. Sneezy
3. Happy
4. Doc
5. Bashful
6. Grumpy
7. Dopey
8. Mickey

Wait a Minute! That list has EIGHT dwarfs on it! Did you read the entire list? If you did, you know that we added *Mickey* on the list of dwarfs. We know he is really a mouse and not really a dwarf. *We just wanted to have a little fun and see if you were paying attention!*

Mickey's PhilharMagic

Mickey's PhilharMagic is a four-dimensional (4-D) musical movie that appeals to all your senses! While there's so much to see and hear, you also get to smell tasty treats and feel a few puffs of air.

Enter the grand concert hall and put on 3-D glasses for this show. Be sure to look all around you—at one point, Donald Duck's Audio-Animatronic rear-end is sticking out of the back wall!

The majority of the show takes place on the huge theater screen. Mickey Mouse and Donald Duck are the stars while Ariel, Aladdin, Jasmine and Simba help to recreate some of the most beloved movie scenes—with a new twist!

Everyone in the family enjoys this fast-paced musical, while being entertained by the characters that pop out of the screen!

Kid's Trivia!

The name PhilharMagic is a play on the real word *philharmonic* which means that a bunch of musicians play their instruments together at the same time.

Kid's Tip!

Make the Seven Dwarfs Mine Train your number one Lightning Lane choice. This is the most popular ride for kids in the Magic Kingdom, so lines are often long! If you do have to wait in line, this is another ride that has a lot of great games and things to see and do while waiting your turn.

Early Priorities

For those who plan to catch Enchanted Tales with Belle, get there first thing. It is really popular and has a slow line. You get to help Belle act out her story with its happy ending!

After reading the rest of this section, you can add other early priorities to your list!

Enchanted Tales with Belle

Beauty and the Beast fans, this is your chance to get up close and personal with Belle as she tells the "tale as old as time." Once you step inside her papa's small cottage, a magical mirror transports you to Beast's castle.

Lumiere, the friendly candlestick from Beauty and the Beast, greets guests before entering the library. Before long, Belle arrives to start telling her story with help from her audience.

Kid's Tip!

Volunteers Wanted! After being introduced to Madame Wardrobe and her assistant, kids (and a couple of parents!) are asked to join in the fun.

If you want a role in the play, wave your hand high in the air! Everyone who wants to take part is included. Even if you don't get a speaking role, make sure you get at least a non-speaking role–only those who participate get to meet Belle and take a picture with her afterward!

This is a popular and fun experience for older kids and parents, too!

HINT: Get a Lightning Lane reservation if you don't want to wait in the long line. It moves very slowly due to the length of each show.

Tomorrowland

Tomorrowland was designed with the future in mind! Imagineers wanted to show guests what the future may look like. It was designed back in the late 1960s, but got a big upgrade in the 1990s. Tomorrowland features technology only dreamed of when it first opened (like rocket ships!).

Tomorrowland Transit Authority PeopleMover

The Tomorrowland Transit Authority "PeopleMover" ("TTA" for short) is a slow-moving form of transportation that gives riders an up-high and inside-the-rides view of the whole land. Magnets move the vehicles, rather than burning fossil fuels. Is this the future of energy conservation?

Kid's Tip!

Take this ride when you first get to Tomorrowland to see how this part of the park is laid out. You can get a good idea of where you want to go next!

On your ride, you'll get a quick peek into Buzz Lightyear's Space Ranger Spin, you'll journey through the dark recesses of Space Mountain, and you'll even see a model of what Walt Disney envisioned EPCOT to look like.

When it's hot outside and your legs are tired, this trip can cool you down a little because it moves fast enough to feel a breeze.

The TTA generally has short lines that move quickly—be sure to try it!

Listen to the announcement, as you zip along the TTA. They are trying to page "Mr. Morrow, Mr. Tom Morrow. Please contact Mr. Johnson in the control tower to confirm your flight to the moon."

Space Mountain

This is one of the *most extreme roller coasters* in Magic Kingdom. There are no inversions (meaning it doesn't go upside down), so it's not too scary. There are fast drops and sharp turns as you zoom around through the dark space. It is so dark inside that you can barely see where you are going, which adds to the fun. You don't need to see in order to hear the special sound effects of other rockets zooming around you.

Sit in the front of the rocket for the wildest ride! With no people in front of you, every dip and turn comes as a complete surprise. In the pitch black, it seems like you are moving really fast. While 28 miles per hour is *kind of fast*, it's not nearly as fast as other roller coasters you get to experience at Disney World. For example, Big Thunder Mountain gets as fast as 35 miles per hour!

Space Mountain might not be good if you are afraid of the dark. The darkness can scare some kids, but it's totally worth it if you can overcome your fear!

Minimum Height Required:
44" tall (3 feet, 8 inches)

HINT: Get Lightning Lane reservations for both Space Mountain and Tron Lightcycle Power Run or visit it first thing in the morning to avoid crowds.

Tron Lightcycle Power Run

Magic Kingdom's other extreme coaster is a high tech ride based on the Tron movies. It's awesome!

Climb onto a lightcycle. (It's basically a futuristic motorcycle you get strapped into.) Take a fast and furious spin around the track.

This is the most intense fun you can have at Magic Kingdom.

This ride is for bigger kids, since they can't safely strap smaller kids into the cycles. If you're tall enough for it, you're going to love it!

Minimum Height Required:
48" tall (4 feet)

Special Boarding Instructions

Due to the crazy popularity of this attraction, Disney uses a brand new virtual queue system for it.

If you don't buy a Lightning Lane reservation for it, you must sign up for a *boarding group* through the My Disney Experience app at 7:00 a.m. the morning you want to go on the ride.

(Tell your parents to start trying early. The virtual queue fills up *within minutes.* If you don't get into the virtual queue or buy a Lightning Lane reservation, there is no way to go on the ride.)

Once your boarding group number is listed as available, you can make your way to the actual queue (and wait in line). This could be several hours later, so you're free to enjoy the rest of the park while you wait for your number to be called!

HINT: Tron is the newest Magic Kingdom ride. Get a Lightning Lane reservation to make sure you get a chance to go on it.

Walt Disney's Carousel of Progress

The Carousel of Progress was introduced to the world by Walt Disney at the 1964 World's Fair in New York City. He considered it one of his favorite attractions!

You're in for a unique ride because the theater moves, while the stage stays in place!

The show progresses through four scenes, traveling through time, each about a generation apart.

Over the past century, a lot of things have changed in our homes. This Audio-Animatronic attraction shows what life was like before a lot of the things came into existence that we now take for granted.

The show *depicts* (shows) family life throughout several decades. Did you know homes did not commonly have indoor plumbing early in the 20th century (the 1900s). Instead, they had to draw water from a well and use an outhouse. Another thing that was not common even 100 years ago was electricity. Without electricity, we could not have television, computers or microwaves.

This attraction was last updated in 1993, so the final peek into "modern technology" is kind of funny. When you see the "new technologies" they show, it makes kids laugh because they are old-fashioned now.

KID'S TRIVIA!

The Carousel of Progress made history. It holds the record of the "longest running stage show, with the most performances, in the history of American theater." Wow!

Don't be surprised if you find yourself singing, "There's a Great, Big, Beautiful Tomorrow" as you exit. This catchy tune plays every time the scenes change.

This attraction is air-conditioned and indoors. It has a fast-moving line, making it great if you want to sit down and relax.

Hidden Mickey Alert!

More than one Hidden Mickey can be found in the Christmas scene. Look at the top of the fireplace mantle to see a Mickey nutcracker.

Buzz Lightyear's Space Ranger Spin

Your mission is to stop the evil Emperor Zurg! He has ordered his robot minions to steal all the batteries from all the friendly toys. They need the batteries to power their ultimate weapon of destruction.

Kid's Tip!

Pay attention to hints in the queue to learn how to get a higher score.

As you board the ride, you enter into a real-life video game and play along with cartoon toys.

You might hear "To infinity and beyond!" more than once while you play.

Buzz drafts you into service as a Junior Space Ranger and you are under his direct command. Use your spinning spaceship to fight Zurg and his robots by firing at them with your laser cannon. A lever on your vehicle controls its movement, allowing you to spin left and right. The targets you want to hit have a big "Z" bulls-eye on them. Each time you hit them, you zap Zurg's energy and gain points.

Your score is recorded on the dashboard to compete against your family, friends, and other players. Top scores are posted on a big scoreboard at the end of the ride! Based on your final score, you are assigned a Ranger Rank.

If you are visiting during a busy time, get a Lightning Lane reservation. Otherwise, visit early in the morning or just keep an eye on the line toward the end of the day!

Kid's Tip!

To get the maximum points, hold the trigger button down the whole time. Aim for smaller and distant targets. They are worth more than larger ones.

Hidden Mickey Alert!

Inside the queue there is a poster on the right wall. The continents on Planet Prime are in the shape of Mickey! During the short movie, watch the planets as they fly by. About halfway through the space video scene, you'll see a Hidden Mickey speed past.

Monsters, Inc. Laugh Floor

The Monsters, Inc. Laugh Floor is a comedy show starring characters from the

Monsters Inc. movies. Mike Wazowski is the "monster of ceremonies." These monsters don't want to make kids scream, instead they want to make everyone laugh. Their goal is to store up all the *laughter* to power the city.

KID'S TRIVIA!

We learned in the Monsters, Inc. movie that laughter gives more power than screams, so the monsters learned how to be funny.

Lucky guests are able to interact with humorous animated friends during their comedy stage show. Some of the audience gets to join in the fun!

You can text jokes directly to Disney while you wait in the queue. If you're lucky, one might even get used during the show!

Astro Orbiter

High above the middle of Tomorrowland is a spaceship ride called Astro Orbiter! It's above the glowing tower called Rockettower—you'll have to take an elevator up to the to the top of the building to reach the ride.

It's really cool to be able to look over all of Magic Kingdom as you soar around colorful planets. This is a spin ride like Dumbo; however, it spins much more quickly! Also like Dumbo, there is a lever to control each ship's up and down movement. Sit in the front if you want the honors!

Kids' Warning! This is a fast ride and kids with a fear of heights won't want to do it.

Be Nice! Please don't ever force someone to go on a ride that they're too scared to enjoy. That's not fun for anyone! Give encouragement. If that doesn't work, just let it go.

Tomorrowland Speedway

In Tomorrowland, you can drive a real race car without a driver's license!

At the Speedway, kids get to drive a gas-powered go-cart that is dressed up to look like an actual NASCAR. That's right kids—YOU get to take the wheel! Take your parents for a drive for once!

You get to drive around a long, winding race track in a car equipped with real steering and braking systems. Don't worry about crashing because the cars run on a metal guide rail that keep them on track. (Definition: A guide rail is a device or mechanism to direct products, vehicles or other objects through a roadway or rail system.)

Little kids love this ride! If your little brother or sister is too short to drive, take them on it for some quality racing time! Even if there is a long line, the Tomorrowland Speedway makes kids happy.

Minimum Height Required:

54" tall (4 feet, 6 inches) to drive the car by yourself;

32" (2 feet, 8 inches) to ride with a taller kid or adult

Entertainment

Shows, parades and other special events are listed on a "Times Guide." The Magic Kingdom has more entertainment listed than all the other parks. Times Guides are available in lots of places: at the park entrance and at any retail location or restaurant. Just ask any Cast Member if you need one!

Casey's Corner Pianist

Right outside Casey's Corner restaurant, a talented musician plays classic tunes on an upright piano. He also plays famous Disney tunes you've heard in movies! One of the pianists is Jim Omohundro who has been playing here for about 40 years! Meet this friendly piano player and ask him to play one of your favorite songs.

Dapper Dans

Main Street's barbershop quartet is a singing group that you can find traveling up and down Main Street, U.S.A. They even have a bicycle made for four aboard which they sometimes perform!

Mickey's Royal Friendship Faire

Mickey's Royal Friendship Faire is a lively, musical show held right in front of Cinderella Castle! Mickey & Minnie host a fun-filled celebration with friends from all over the kingdom. Sing and dance along with Mickey Mouse, Donald Duck, Elsa, Rapunzel, Tiana and all their friends! This show takes place several times daily.

Festival of Fantasy Parade

During this popular, afternoon parade, favorite Disney characters pass by on larger-than-life parade floats. Wave to Anna and Elsa and other *Frozen* characters, as well as Peter Pan, Ariel, Cinderella and so many more! Be sure to look for the real fire-breathing dragon!

Plan ahead and find a good spot to watch on the curb anywhere along the major roads (promenades) at least 30 minutes before the parade begins. This parade is so amazing that everyone wants to see it, and it's smart to find good spots really early.

This parade takes place once a day in the afternoon. (Check the Times Guide for the exact time.)

Royal Majesty Makers

This is a smaller parade through Fantasyland and you can join in! Young princes and princesses greet their subjects after getting dressed up in their finery. (A visit to Bibbidi Bobbidi Boutique beforehand will get you prepared, but you can also dress up at home!)

Move It! Shake It! Dance & Play It! Street Party

Get ready to Dance! This hoppin' parade turns into a dance party at the hub in front of Cinderella Castle. You'll get a chance to dance and jump around with Mickey and Minnie Mouse, Donald Duck, Stitch, and even Chip and Dale!

This exciting street party lasts 35 minutes and typically occurs 3 times throughout the day!

Cosmic Dance Party

Can't get enough dancing? Check out the Cosmic Dance Party that occurs most nights at Rockettower Plaza Stage in Tomorrowland. (Keep in mind it's only open "weather-permitting" which means that if it rains, the show is canceled.)

Dancing Fun! Additional dancing opportunities. Other than the dance party above, there are a couple other places where you can shake your bootie!

- Disney Springs - Dance to DJ Music
- Hollywood Studios - Disney Junior Live on Stage

Happily Ever After Nighttime Show

Scenes and songs from Disney movies take over Cinderella Castle and the night sky above.

The **Happily Ever After** fireworks show illuminates both the castle and the sky over Cinderella Castle in the middle of the park! Lasers and projections play scenes of friendship, love and heroic adventure all over the castle and down Main Street.

The best place to watch both shows is in the middle of Main Street facing toward the castle. Be sure to catch a glimpse of Tinker Bell flying from the castle to Tomorrowland!

Magic Kingdom Rides

I	H	E	S	I	U	R	C	E	L	G	N	U	J
B	A	R	N	S	T	O	R	M	E	R	N	B	N
R	U	U	M	A	A	R	E	B	E	I	I	R	T
M	N	I	A	R	S	T	O	T	N	T	A	T	N
D	T	M	D	E	T	N	O	N	D	A	T	I	M
U	E	N	T	D	R	I	T	R	I	E	N	I	L
M	D	E	E	N	O	T	B	T	M	I	U	S	R
B	M	R	A	U	O	N	N	O	E	O	O	T	H
O	A	H	P	H	R	R	A	S	I	E	M	A	U
T	N	B	A	T	B	P	R	E	E	O	E	A	A
A	S	Y	R	G	I	A	C	E	O	I	C	O	A
E	I	I	T	I	T	U	E	C	D	A	A	R	E
M	O	N	Y	B	E	N	U	M	A	N	P	J	A
T	N	T	H	M	R	P	L	O	I	E	S	R	O

BARNSTORMER
BIG THUNDER
JUNGLE CRUISE
HAUNTED MANSION
TRON
SPACE MOUNTAIN
DUMBO
ASTRO ORBITER
MAD TEA PARTY

Character Meet & Greets

Meet a Disney Star

Even though you can see them in parades and shows, you can meet some favorite characters in person and get a photograph and autograph! Here is a sample list of who might be available on the day of your visit.

Remember, available characters change regularly. Check the Times Guide when you get to the park to see who is waiting to meet you that day!

Character	***Location***
Alice in Wonderland characters	Fantasyland
Aladdin and Jasmine	Adventureland (near the magic carpet ride
Ariel (The Little Mermaid)	Ariel's Grotto in Fantasyland
Buzz Lightyear	Tomorrowland
Gaston	Near Gaston's Tavern in Fantasyland
Main Street Citizens (Magic Kingdom Mayor, etc.)	Main Street, U.S.A.
Merida	Fairytale Garden (near Cinderella Castle)
Mickey Mouse	Town Square Theater
Minnie, Daisy, Donald & Goofy	Pete's Silly Sideshow in Storybook Circus
Miscellaneous Characters	Town Square and Main Street, U.S.A.
Peter Pan	Near Peter Pan's Flight in Fantasyland
Princesses: Cinderella, Elena, Rapunzel & Tiana	Princess Fairytale Hall in Fantasyland
Tigger & Winnie the Pooh	Near The Many Adventures of Winnie the Pooh in Fantasyland
Tinker Bell	Town Square Theater

Disney Princesses

Across

2. Don't mess with this princess who has been to war.
4. _______ White was the first Disney princess.
5. This princess dreams of a life on land.
7. She knows how to get down and dirty with a mop.
9. Don't cut her really long hair!

Down

1. She'll make you see the "Colors of the Wind."
3. The sea called out to this princess.
5. She met her true love and prince, before she even knew she was a princess.
6. The only way to her heart is through a library.
8. Only her sister, the Queen, could save her from a cold spell.

*Answers on Page 210

ATTRACTION RATINGS

Super Cool (MUST-SEE)	Cool (SHOULD SEE)	Fun (SEE IF YOU CAN)
Space Mountain	Jungle Cruise	it's a small world
Seven Dwarfs Mine Train	Monster's, Inc. Laugh Floor	Country Bear Jamboree
Big Thunder Mountain Railroad	Tom Sawyer Island	Tomorrowland PeopleMover
Tiana's Bayou Adventure	Mickey's PhilharMagic	Liberty Belle Riverboat
Enchanted Tales with Belle	Prince Charming Regal Carrousel	Frontierland Shootin' Arcade
Peter Pan's Flight	Mad Tea Party	Walt Disney's Enchanted Tiki Room
The Haunted Mansion	The Barnstormer	The Hall of Presidents
Pirates of the Caribbean	Astro Orbiter	Swiss Family Treehouse
Buzz Lightyear Space Ranger Spin	The Magic Carpets of Aladdin	Walt Disney's Carousel of Progress
Under the Sea – Journey of the Little Mermaid	Walt Disney World Railroad	
Tomorrowland Speedway	Festival of Fantasy Parade	
Tron Lightcycle Power Run		
The Many Adventures of Winnie the Pooh		
Dumbo the Flying Elephant		
Disney Enchantment		

Let's Go to Epcot!

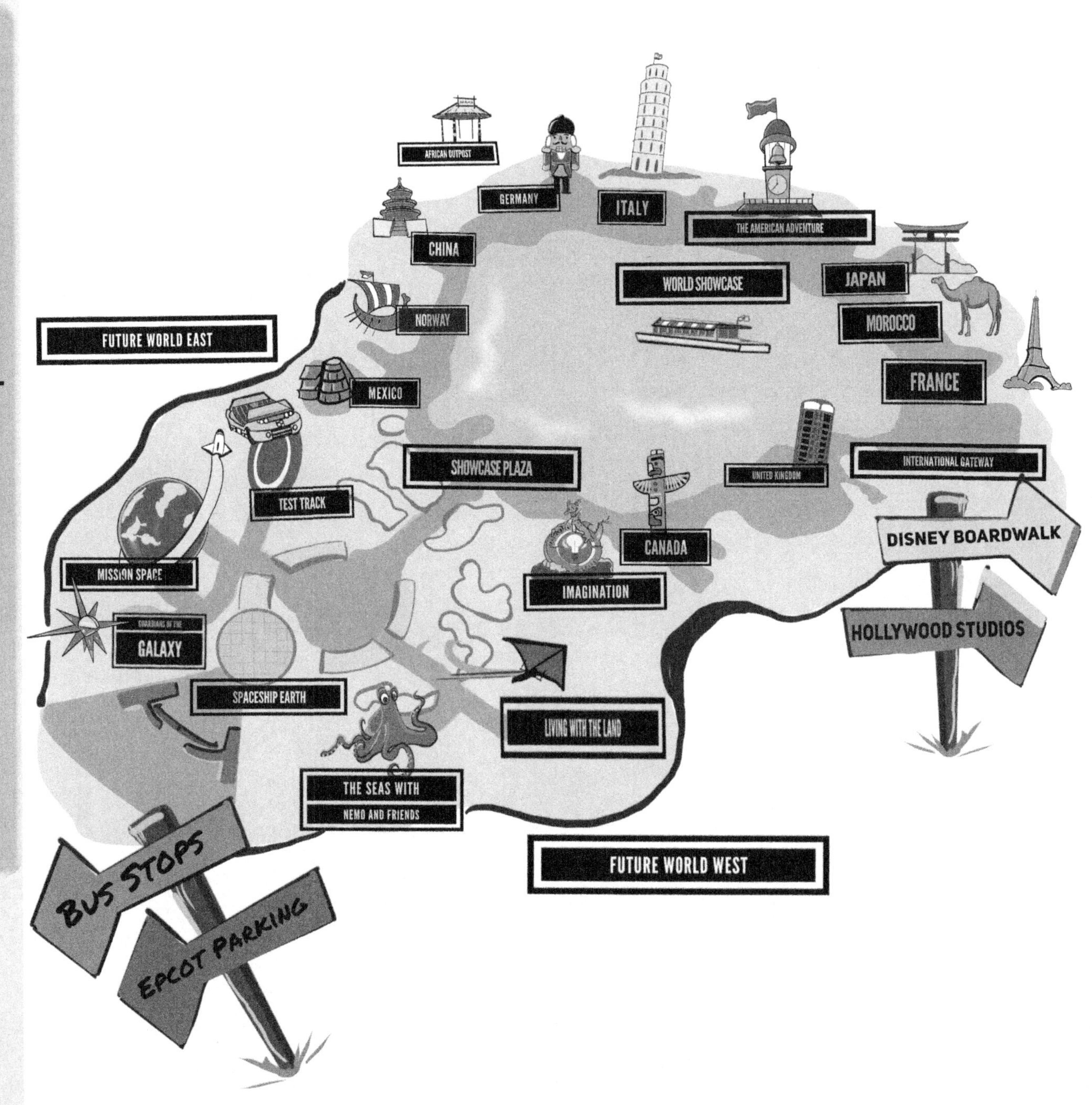

Let your inner genius and explorer out! Discover new, inspiring ideas and inventions at Disney World's second park, Epcot (which stands for Experimental Prototype Community of Tomorrow). It is committed to diversity (meaning a wide variety) of world cultures, imagination and innovation.

Walt Disney wanted Epcot to be the "City of the Future." His early plans were for a real, self-contained community to be developed. Walt died in 1966 long before this park was built. While it has changed from the original vision, designers keep the spirit of learning and exploring alive.

Kid's Tip!

Take a short journey on Magic Kingdom's Tomorrowland Transit Authority. It's a train-like ride that lets you catch a glimpse of Mr. Disney's initial, miniature model of Epcot. It was planned as an actual *community* where people would live and work.

Epcot History. Epcot opened to the public October 1, 1982, although the official opening ceremony came 23 days later, on October 24.

The park was originally split into two super-fun areas, each different and distinct. There's a fun story behind how that happened.

During the design phase, Imagineers argued over two different visions for the new theme park. John Hench, a Disney Imagineer, had to come up with a solution to make everyone happy.

One day, miniature models of both parks were laying on a table in the design room. He simply pushed them together and asked, "How about this?!"

Rather than settling on a single concept and disappointing the losing design team, everyone agreed on the final decision: "Let's do both!"

From that point on, Epcot was split into Future World and World Showcase. Separating them with a large lake seemed like the right thing to do.

The first area (Future World) was all about new technology, human achievement and scientific innovation. It focused on many things:

- Technological achievements in science, industry and imagination;
- Discovery of ideas and inventions;
- Transportation, energy, telecommunications and computer technology;
- Science and exploration of land, skies, seas and outer space.

Epcot Today. Epcot has had a lot of updates in recent years. Along some really great new rides, Disney decided to give it a more unified theme.

The two areas are now split into four neighborhoods.

What used to be Future World is now known for its three *distinct* (meaning you can recognize that it's different) neighborhoods: World Celebration, World Discovery, and World Nature.

These neighborhood names really describe the focus of each.

World Showcase is the fourth neighborhood. It celebrates the culture, cuisine and sights of different countries around the globe. Centered around a lagoon, World Showcase represents 11 countries - each with its own pavilion.

Kid's Tip!

Buildings and lands are called "*pavilions*" (pronounced "puh-vill-yuhnz").

You can walk through the four neighborhoods and around the promenade.

You can also take one of two boats that travel back and forth across the lagoon until dusk, the time that the sun sets in the evening.

Kid's Tip!

World Celebration, Discovery, and Nature at Epcot have small crowds in the evening. Go back there after 3:00 p.m. to do anything you missed earlier in the day.

Harmonious. Experience everything you love about Disney music in this exciting nighttime fireworks show!

Lasers, music and fireworks light up the lagoon. Pay attention to the spinning globe. The show highlights how music inspires people across the globe!

It starts at 9:00 p.m. most evenings and can be viewed from locations all around the World Showcase Lagoon.

World Celebration Highlights	Shops (Mouse Gear & Club Cool) Spaceship Earth The Imagination Pavilion - with Figment!
World Discovery Highlights	Guardians of the Galaxy: Cosmic Rewind Mission: SPACE Test Track
World Nature Highlights	The Land Pavilion - Soarin' Around the World The Seas Pavilion - See Nemo & Friends
World Showcase Highlights	Visit international countries See cool buildings Listen to unique sounds Learn foreign language
World Showcase Attractions	Duck Tales World Showcase Adventure Frozen Ever After Remy's Ratatouille Adventure The Three Caballeros
Things to Consider	Think about what life would be like in each country. What would you love about it? What would you not like so much?

Kid's Tip!

Try to find a spot to watch the fireworks on the steps leading to the Canada pavilion. You get a great view of the show!

World Celebration

When you first enter the park from the front, you are in World Celebration. This is where the big silver ball is. (We tell you all about this giant "geosphere" in a bit!)

World Celebration allows families to focus on Invention and Imagination while having fun! Explore your imagination through the senses, take a ride inside Spaceship Earth, check out the innovation behind EPCOT and more!

World Nature

To the right of the entrance, discover World Nature - home to pavilions featuring our land and seas!

Did you know there are gigantic 5.7 million gallon saltwater aquariums filled with over 6,000 sea creatures (representing 60 species) in the Seas with Nemo & Friends Pavilion?! You not only learn about all of this sea life, but you also get to enjoy two awesome attractions: The Seas with Nemo & Friends and Turtle Talk with Crush.

Head to The Land Pavilion to learn how farmers grow food for us to eat on the Living with the Land ride. Did you know Disney grows its own vegetables inside The Land Pavilion and serves these healthy foods to visitors like you in many of its restaurants?

World Discovery

The third neighborhood is the most exciting. Looking for an out of this world ride? Test your outer space knowledge and mechanical skills on Mission: SPACE!

Better yet, take a wild ride on Guardians of the Galaxy: Cosmic Rewind. It's one of the world's longest indoor roller coasters. It starts off with a backwards launch!

These three neighborhoods at the front of the park include other fun rides, too. Create your own race car and ride in it at Test Track, then fly high above the globe at Soarin' Around the World. Travel through the history of our planet in Spaceship Earth. Other attractions include The Disney & Pixar Short Film Festival and Journey Into Imagination with Figment.

World Showcase

Take a world tour with realistic experiences of foreign cultures and traditions.

As you journey around World Showcase, there is lots to see and do. The buildings look just like the real ones from each country, and they even have authentic street performances!

Discover all the art and history that you probably didn't know. World Showcase teaches you about great cities of the world, as well as what the relaxing countryside is like through the films you can view.

World Showcase even has street entertainment and shows. There is so much to observe!

Kid's Tip!

Belly dancers entertain families inside Restaurant Marrakesh in Morocco; Germany's Biergarten restaurant has a live oompah band; and you can meet princesses at Akershus restaurant in Norway!

Let's go on a ride!

Both Mexico and Norway have fun boat rides. The most popular ride is the fabulous *Remy's Ratatouille Adventure* in the France pavilion!

Great Films!

Four pavilions have exciting movies that share important history, cultural traditions and scenery from each country. These are shown throughout the day in four pavilions: The American Adventure, China, Canada and France. (Plus there's a fun Beauty & the Beast sing-a-long movie in France!)

Authentic Buildings!

Discover 11 different nations. Each is showcased with buildings and landmarks that look just like the real ones in each country (just smaller)! The architecture (which means building designs) and detailed landscaping in each pavilion makes you feel like you are traveling to foreign lands.

Some areas are designed to look like museums; other places allow you to sit back and enjoy time with your friends and family.

Kidcot Fun Stops are Just for Kids!

There are places called Kidcot Fun Stops in each country pavilion. All kids can have fun there and bring something special home. You get a neat pack with a special card in each country. Hand color it with crayons or markers. Each pack has information about what makes that country special. In each Kidcot area, you can chat with the Cast Members (Disney employees). Ask them what kids do to have fun in their home countries!

Most Cast Members you find in each pavilion are native to that country. Don't be afraid to say Hello - these Cast Members are eager to teach you a word or two in their language or answer any questions you have about their culture. Ask them about themselves. We all like to tell our own story. Maybe they want you to share yours!

Kid's Tip!

Ask Cast Members in China, Japan and Morocco to write your name in their language!

Foreign Language Fun!

Here is how you say hello in each of the foreign languages you encounter:

Land (Language)	
France (French)	Bon jour ("bawn-zhoor") means good day in French and is how they say hello.
Morocco (Arabic)	Salaam alaikum ("saw-lawm-a-LAY-koom") means hello in Arabic.
Italy (Italian)	Buongiorno ("bon Jor-no") means good day in Italian and is how they say hello.
Germany (German)	Guten Tag! ("GOOT-in Tahg") means good day and is how Germans say hello.
China (Chinese)	Ni Hao ("nee-how") means hello.
Norway (Norwegian)	God dag ("goo dog") [the g in the word god is silent] means good day and is how Norwegians say hello.
Mexico (Spanish)	Hola ("OH-law") means hello in Spanish.
Japan (Japanese)	Ohayo gozaimasu ("oh-high-oh goh-za-ee-mahs") means good morning in Japanese and is a common greeting.

If you want, you can ask them how to say other words and phrases. You can ask them to tell you how they spell and pronouce things like

How Are You? Thank You!
Good Bye! My name is…

Write down their answers here!

English Phrase or Word	Country/Language	Translation

Let's Go to Epcot!

There are many restaurants offering authentic cuisine (food) throughout the 11 countries. These restaurants show off culture and traditions. Best of all, the food tastes great!

Meet Real Foreigners!

Strike up a conversation with the international Cast Members from each country; ask them to teach you a word or two of their language and some fun facts about their culture. They love to talk about their homelands, and you can impress your family and friends with your knowledge!

Most countries in World Showcase have beautiful courtyards. Courtyards or city squares are enchanting places where town folks in each country historically spent their evenings. It would usually be close to the church.

Go inside the giant pyramid in the Mexico Pavilion. There's a boat ride where you chase Donald Duck as he travels through Mexico. (Look for the active volcano nearby!) In Germany, find the miniature trains that pass through a tiny mountain village. Did you see the gondolas in Italy?

There are prayer temples in China, and religious buildings in Japan, too.

Where can you find the Eiffel tower? In France, but of course!

The America pavilion is host to all the other nations (because Disney World is in America). This is why it sits smack-dab-in-the-middle of World Showcase with its grand colonial building!

Did you know? World Showcase was originally designed to increase tourism to each represented land, so the countries actually paid to take part. Most also helped design the pavilions to keep them authentic.

World Celebration Attractions

Spaceship Earth

Before your car or bus is even parked, a giant silver dome that kind of looks like a golf ball may catch your eye. (It's called a geodesic — pronounced "jee-oh-dee-sik" — sphere or geosphere.) This is Epcot's park icon. Because it stands 180 feet tall, it can be seen from just about anywhere you're standing in Epcot.

Inside this sphere is a fun ride called Spaceship Earth. The best view of Spaceship Earth is right when you enter the front of the park.

Did You Know? Spaceship Earth is the world's largest free-standing (meaning not attached to another building) sphere. However, it is actually oblong - therefore not a perfect, round sphere. Its estimated weight is a whopping 16 million pounds!

As you board the ride, a touch screen on the dashboard of your ride vehicle lets you choose options for a fun video that you get to watch later on.

Kid's Tip!

Take off your hat and make a silly face when your picture is taken at the beginning of the ride. It will pay off when you see the video later!

Did You Know? While Spaceship Earth is a Geodesic Sphere - it actually contains two spheres - one inside the other! The inner sphere contains the ride; the outer sphere is a shell designed for rainwater to gather into a gutter system, rather than streaming down the sides onto guests below.

Rain is actually absorbed through the outer sphere through small openings in the surface, and the water is then channeled into the World Showcase lagoon through the gutter system. Now that's cool!

Throughout the ride, the narrator explains how people influenced the history of innovations and technology. Learn how our methods of communication have advanced throughout the years.

This is the first ride people see when they enter the park, so **it usually takes longer to get on the ride first thing rather than later in the day.** Come back in the late afternoon or early evening to go on this with little to no wait.

Don't wait in a long line, but definitely see this once!

Project Tomorrow: Inventing the Wonders of the Future

After you exit Spaceship Earth, you arrive at the "Project Tomorrow" area, which is full of fun, interactive exhibits. Look up on the screen map of the world to see your picture from the ride! Visit a kiosk to email your ride video to a friend, discover current medical diagnostics for your home, play a driving simulation game and more!

Imagination

The Imagination Pavilion contains many hands-on attractions designed to make you think through play! Check out the Disney & Pixar Short Film Festival showing entertaining cartoons (plus, it allows everyone to rest their feet!).

Enjoy the Leap Frog Fountains - jumping water that actually flows upwards, over your head as you walk down the sidewalk.

Journey Into Imagination with Figment

Take a tour through the Imagination Institute with Figment, the friendly purple dragon. He'll teach you about the five senses, in his own special and silly way!

ImageWorks

As you exit your tour with Figment, you enter into the ImageWorks "What If" labs. This is the place where many young kids spend a lot of time, because there are so many hands-on (and feet-on!) activities! Take a few minutes and play with an electric philharmonic that lets you conduct your own orchestra by waving your hands in the air. (The musical instruments actually respond to your motion!) There is also a kiosk where you can send a special email message to let your friends back home see the fun you're having. (Have their email addresses handy.)

Epcot Character Spot

Meet some of your favorite characters inside one of two buildings at Epcot Character Spot. On one side, meet Mickey, Minnie and Goofy; on the other, meet Baymax, Joy and Sadness (depending on which queue you enter).

Outside, you can find Chip 'n' Dale throughout much of the day. Remember to check your Times Guide to find out when all of the characters will be greeting guests!

Club Cool

Need a cool drink on a hot day? Head to Club Cool for free (yes, free!) soda samples from across the globe. Find out what kids like you drink in far-away countries like Japan and Italy.

World Nature Attractions

The Seas with Nemo & Friends (The Seas Pavilion)

The Seas with Nemo & Friends Ride

Climb aboard your clammobile to join a class trip headed by Nemo's school teacher, Mr. Ray.

Nemo has wandered away from the rest of the class and you get to help his dad and friends (Dory, Bruce, Crush, Chum and Squirt) find him!

There are many scenes that are familiar from the movie, including a voyage through jellyfish and riding the EAC (East Australian Current) with Crush. (A *current* is water that flows in the same direction.)

Near the ride's end, special effects make it look like the cartoon sea creatures are swimming with real fish in an aquarium.

The exit takes you to an amazing aquarium full of marine life!

Turtle Talk with Crush

Turtle Talk with Crush is a totally tubular, live show where the cartoon character on the screen really talks to members of the audience. Even your parents are going to laugh hysterically!

Sea Base

More than 4,000 real sea creatures are found in the huge aquarium and smaller water tanks for hands-on fun and exploration. Meet disabled manatees that have been rescued from the wild. See real sharks, seahorses, angelfish, dolphins, stingrays, sea turtles and so much more! Fish feedings occur daily at 10 AM and 3:30 PM - it's a sight to see!

On **Level 1** of the Sea Base is the Nemo and Friends! exhibit. Search for clownfish, blue tangs, starfish, seahorses and stingrays. You can also view the *Can you Find Nemo?* habitat, check out the Great Barrier Reef display, observe the stingray habitat Mr. Ray's Lagoon and look at jellyfish! It's a simple exhibit, but definitely worth seeing.

This is a real, working marine research center. On **Level 2**, there is an Observation Deck where scheduled activities go on throughout the day. You can visit the manatees on the 2nd level as well. These manatees have been rescued and are going through rehabilitation before being released back into the wild. Be sure to view the short manatee videos on the TVs overhead - worth the watch! Finally, there is an Ocean Resource Exhibit about the farming of aquatic plants.

Did You Know? 5.7 million gallons of water fill the aquarium tank. There are 56 giant windows for viewing. When the tank was filled with water, 27 truckloads of salt had to be delivered and added to the water in order to make the salt water that the fish needed to survive and live in the environment. It's so big that Spaceship Earth could be fully submerged into the Seas aquarium.

Before leaving the pavilion, be sure to check out *Bruce's Shark World*. This play area teaches about these scary-looking ocean predators. There's even a giant set of shark teeth that you can take your photo in. Kids who like the sea and animals can spend a long time exploring the pavilion!

The Land

Hidden Mickey Alert!

Look in the cloud under the blue balloon flying in the sky in the center of the pavilion.

Located next door is a building called *The Land*. Its roof gives away the fact that it contains a giant greenhouse and a hint of what is highlighted inside. This pavilion includes two rides, a show and two restaurants.

Living with the Land

While on board this gentle, yet informative, boat ride, learn where food comes from and how it is grown. A narrator explains everything you see.

Many different areas of the world can be observed, such as rain forests, deserts and prairie landscapes.

For the second half of the ride, the boat floats through a modern greenhouse which uses state-of-the-art growing techniques. Don't expect much excitement on this attraction, but there are some neat things to see.

Did You Know? An average of 30 tons of fruits and vegetables are grown per year right from *The Land*. These gardens aren't just for show - they actually provide produce to various restaurants throughout Epcot (like the Garden Grill and Sunshine Seasons). So, if it's fresh fruits and vegetables you're looking for… Epcot is the place to be!

Did you Know? People eat more bananas than any other fruit!

Hidden Mickey Alert!

Look at the bubbles in paintings as you wait in line.

Soarin' Around the World

Buckle up and away you go! In this attraction, guests are seated in a giant hang glider that holds many people.

Soarin' is a unique ride that takes you on a simulated (meaning it seems real, but isn't) hang-gliding trip across the globe. Fly high in the sky above the mountains and down low, nearly touching water as you view some of the most iconic sights in our world: pyramids, the Great Wall of China, the Eiffel Tower, Sydney, and more! Your hang-gliding adventure ends as you finally return home to Epcot.

Soarin' was filmed using special cameras mounted on airplanes and helicopters. It feels like you're really hang-gliding, tilting back and forth. There are even scents and breezes to convince you that you're flying during this five-minute ride!

The "hang-gliding" has a calm motion with effects that most people find exhilarating, and not at all scary.

Motion sickness affects a few people on this attraction. If you start to feel woozy, close your eyes and count to 100. By then, the ride is over!

If you have seen this in the past, the movie was changed in 2016—and it is just as much fun, if not more!

Minimum Height Required:
40" tall (3 feet, 4 inches)

World Discovery Attractions

Guardians of the Galaxy: Cosmic Rewind

This is one of the world's longest enclosed coasters! Go on an exciting journey through the world of Xander and discover its technologies.

Experience Disney's first ever reverse-launch coaster. Hang on tights, as you feel your ride vehicle rotate a full 360 degrees! While this ride is labeled "family friendly" it may be a little too intense for your younger brother or sister.

Minimum Height Required:
42" tall (3 feet, 6 inches)

Journey of Water, Inspired by Moana

Do you love Moana? Take a walk through a water garden that was inspired by her! This walk-through attraction is both educational and fun.

Learn the lifecycle of water and how it's a vital part of the environment. During your trek, you can actually play with interactive water features.

Keep a close eye on the rock formations. You may discover some familiar faces from the film, *Moana*.

This experience is at your own pace, meaning you can go as fast or slow as you want! There usually isn't a wait to get in, but Epcot may make you join a virtual queue for it if it's a really busy day. Tell your parents to check the My Disney Experience app the morning of your visit to see if a virtual queue is in effect and to join it.

Mission: SPACE

Discover your inner astronaut on a special mission. This awesome simulator ride takes you on a journey, either right here on Earth or to the planet Mars! This attraction is especially cool, since real NASA astronauts and engineers helped design it.

Blast off in a rocket ship that holds four crew members with important – and fun! – jobs to do. What role do you want to play?

- Commander (captain)
- Engineer
- Navigator
- Pilot

Two Teams - Green or Orange? At the beginning, you get to choose which team you are on. One team takes you on a ride that is a lot more intense than the other. Members who are a little more daring can opt to join the Orange Team. Their harder mission includes a lot more bouncing and spinning. The Green Team takes you on a smoother, easy mission. It is a good choice if you think you might feel woozy (like you are car sick) or want to avoid a bumpy journey.

What's the ride like? There are four people aboard each mission - each with a different role. Get strapped into a seat and await the instructions from an astronaut (space explorer) of NASA (National Aeronautics and Space Administration). You must carry out those instructions (button pushing, mainly) in order to complete this mission to outer space. (Don't worry, even if you just sit there without pushing the buttons on your control panel, the ride continues.)

Many people find this ride fast and fun - especially during *take-off*! The powerful pull of gravity can be felt during the full minute that it takes to break through Earth's atmosphere. The mission gets smoother for the journey to Mars, but expect to encounter some landing problems.

Kid's Tip!

If you aren't sure which side to ride on Mission: SPACE, choose the Green Team. If you don't get sick, try the Orange Team later. Whatever you do, don't go on the ride if you just ate something!

If you choose the Orange side, expect a lot of bouncing around and spinning. There are some hard bumps and jolts, and it's possible you may feel woozy, especially if you are prone to motion sickness. If you have a fear of small, enclosed spaces (this is called claustrophobia), you may not want to ride.

Even if this attraction is too much for you, you can explore the cool pavilion. There's an entire model of the universe in huge structures outside.

Minimum Height Required:

44" tall (3 feet, 8 inches) for the Orange Team;

40" tall (3 feet, 4 inches) for the Green Team

Advanced Training Lab

Even if riding *Mission: Space!* isn't something you want to do (or you have younger siblings who can't yet ride), you can explore the Advanced Training Lab at the ride exit! This interactive play area is fun for all ages.

Just walk into the *Mission: Space!* exit door to find it. There are a lot of out-of-this-world activities and fun things to do there, and you don't have to go on the ride to experience them!

Crawl through wormholes in the interactive playground. Play digital games and send video postcards to friends back home!

Test Track

This is your chance to design and test a race car! Test Track is one of the fastest rides at Walt Disney World. The fun begins before you even get on the ride. While you wait your turn, you get to design your very own race car on a touch screen, which provides lots of really cool options. Choose your options carefully. During the ride, your car is graded based on its efficiency, power, capability and responsiveness.

After your car is designed, hop aboard your self-driving car! Your ride vehicle contains audio and video that explains how real cars are tested for performance.

The car you ride in looks like all the others, but if you scan your magic band or ticket before getting on the ride, it remembers the race car you designed. Monitors throughout the ride show images of it and compare its performance to the other passengers' designs.

At the end of the ride, you find out whose car had the best overall performance. The winner gets all the bragging rights!

This fun ride zips along the track and around curves, bounces along the bumpy road, and even comes to a screeching halt as the brakes are tested to see how well they work!

After you nearly run into a truck (whew!), your car goes outdoors. This is where you really pick up speed around an oval track. If you are wearing a hat or ears, make sure to take them off before you go outdoors, because your car is going to reach incredible speeds. Be sure to check out the speedometer sign that shows you just how fast your car is driving!

Test Track can be loud at times, but most kids find it fun and not at all scary.

Kid's Tip!

If you have long hair, put it in a ponytail to keep it from getting tangled.

After you exit your car, there is a big area with actual Chevrolet cars you can check out and explore. Seriously, open a car door and climb on in! This is a fun area with great photo opportunities and other fun things to do. If you have a brother or sister too small to ride Test Track, they can hang out in this area and have a ton of fun with Mom or Dad while you ride.

Minimum Height Required:
40" tall (3 feet, 4 inches)

Cool Wash

This outdoor area looks like a car wash, but it sprays a cool water mist. Everyone loves to walk through it and cool off on a hot day. You can sometimes buy cool, refreshing drinks here, like Coca Cola slushies.

World Showcase Attractions

Be a world traveler! See what real towns look like in different countries all over the world, and meet real people who are from those places. They all speak their native tongue (language) and English, but they may have a thick accent that makes them sound different.

While traveling around World Showcase, learn about the history and cultures of different countries and see what makes them proud. Experience the sights and sounds of each country. You can even taste the food!

Want more excitement? Fight villains with your favorite Duck Tales friends in an interactive adventure! And be sure to watch the special entertainment in each country.

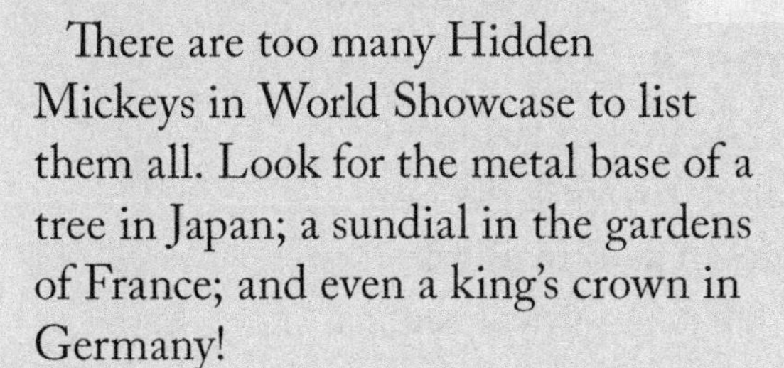

Hidden Mickey Alert!

There are too many Hidden Mickeys in World Showcase to list them all. Look for the metal base of a tree in Japan; a sundial in the gardens of France; and even a king's crown in Germany!

Kid's Tip!

Stop at Guest Relations for interesting fact sheets about the countries!

Did You Know?

Mickey Mouse is an International Superstar

While everyone knows who Mickey Mouse is, not everyone calls him by that name. Check out what everyone's favorite mouse is known as in different countries.

Country	Name
Greece	Miky Maoye
Italy	Topolino
Norway	Mikke Mus
Sweden	Musse Pigg
China	Mi Lao Shu

Canada

Canada is the northernmost country in the western hemisphere, located just above the United States. Canada is known for its beautiful, pristine (meaning clean and unchanged) countrysides as well as its mountaintops.

While exploring the Canada pavilion in Epcot, be sure to check out its Totem poles and First Nation artifacts. Inside the pavilion, you can watch a Movie called *Canada: Far and Wide* that has scenes that completely surround you (yep - it's a *Circle-Vision*, 360-degree theater!). While standing, turn around to see the changing scenery. Be careful, the movie can make you dizzy!

Kid's Tip!

Only one of the two totem poles in Canada is authentic. The real one (carved by a Native American artist) is the more serious and plain totem, while the one created by Disney Imagineers is more cartoon-like and vivid. The authentic totem pole tells a story of the legendary raven from Native American folklore.

United Kingdom

The United Kingdom pavilion features buildings found in London and countryside towns. You can listen to live rock and roll music in an outdoor park, which looks a lot like the famous Hyde Park in London.

Getting a picture inside a red telephone booth is really popular. Be sure to keep an eye out for the red post boxes, chimneys that look like they are really being used, and thatched roof buildings that look like they are made out of hay (really plastic broom bristles).

Be on your best behavior for a "proper" meeting with Mary Poppins and Alice (in Wonderland). Both can be found in the courtyard throughout the day.

Did you know? Epcot is known for its pretty plants and flowers, including very special topiary trees and shrubs during their annual festivals. Topiaries (pronounced "TOE-pea-air-eez") are grown around a metal frame and formed to look like Disney animals and cartoon characters.

Horticulturists (plant specialists) carefully trim each topiary to maintain its exact shape. They use flowers and other plants to give specific textures and colors, which almost bring them to life!

New topiaries are designed and displayed each year as part of the Flower and Garden Festival (an event that takes place every March through May).

Near France, you will find the very popular *Beauty & The Beast* topiary. Sometimes *Captain Hook* and *Tik-Tok* (the crocodile) are in the United Kingdom. Look for *Lion King* characters by the African Outpost.

There are over 200 topiaries found throughout the WDW Resort. While most can be found at Epcot during the Flower & Garden Festival, others can be found all around Disney World year round. For example, a Mary Poppins bush is usually kept at the Grand Floridian resort.

France

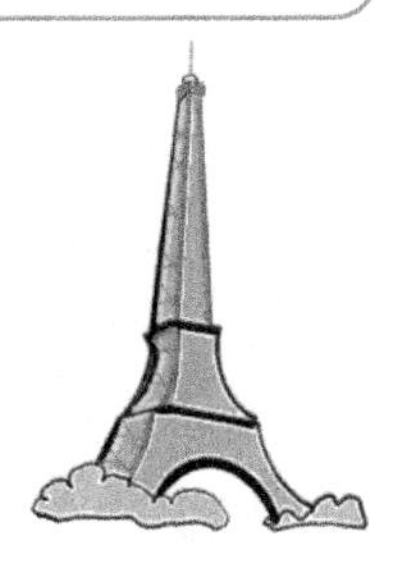

Located in Paris, the Eiffel Tower is the best-known icon in all of France. A perfect replica (copy) towers high overhead at the France pavilion in Epcot!

While visiting the France pavilion, be sure to check out the treats in the bakery, look over the flavors in the ice cream store, and smell all the scents in the perfume shop (or look for the nearest door if the smell is too much).

One of the best parts of France is the shows. There's a great *Beauty and the Beast Sing-Along* film. In it, Mrs. Potts tells a secret backstory you never knew before!

The sing-a-long is in an air-conditioned theater that sometimes shows another film, called *Impressions de France* — that means Impressions of France in English. The movie shows scenes from all across the country, including the big cities and the idyllic countryside.

Since both shows share a theater, check the Times Guide to see when each one is showing on the day you visit. Try to see them both!

If you head over to the garden, you might get to meet Aurora there. Belle is also sometimes down by the lagoon. Check your Times Guide when you arrive at Epcot to find out when each will be available for a meet-and-greet.

Remy's Ratatouille Adventure

Be on the lookout for an even more exciting experience. France has Epcot's most popular attraction, *Remy's Ratatouille Adventure.*

This exciting ride uses the latest 4-D, smooth track technology to make it super fun and unique. Shrink to the size of a rat and try to help Remy make a dish, as you zip along on a whacky trip through one of Paris' nicest restaurants. Don't get caught!

Kingdom of Morocco

Morocco is one of the most immersive pavilions at Epcot. The king of Morocco wanted to make sure every detail was perfect, so visitors can experience what it is actually like in Morocco. During the construction of this pavilion, he sent his own builders and artists to Disney to get every detail absolutely perfect!

Within the Morocco pavilion there are bright and beautiful mosaics – artwork made from little ceramic tiles. Notice the patterns - there are no images of people or animals, because you would never find designs like that in Morocco.

The pavilion takes you through the country's most famous cities of Fez and Marrakesh. As you walk by, stop and enjoy the live Moroccan band along the promenade (walkway).

Listen for sounds of shopkeepers and breath deeply to take in the scents as you walk through the Bazaar. Its many shops sell real Moroccan items like jewelry, sandals, clothing, fez (type of hat), brass items and more!

Jasmine is also waiting inside the Bazaar to meet you. Check the Times Guide for her scheduled appearances.

The Marrakesh restaurant is one of the most unique places to eat in all of Walt Disney World. The food is great and you get to watch a real belly dancer while you grab a bite to eat.

Interested in extreme running races? Check out the Gallery of Arts and History and learn about two modern-day races that take place in Morocco! There's more to see than just art work — check out the floor tiles and lighting fixtures too!

Did you know? The Kingdom of Morocco was the first nation to formally recognize the newly-formed United States of America as a sovereign (possessing supreme or ultimate power) nation after the Revolutionary War.

Japan

Walking to Japan, a giant temple immediately catches your eye. It's called a pagoda and looks just like the real one in the city of Nara.

While you're there, be sure to catch the Japanese drummers perform! If you like to shop, go inside the pavilion to browse through a huge department store with many items found in Japan. There's even a place you can choose an oyster to get a real pearl! Have fun checking out all the authentic Japanese candy, too.

Did you know? Mark Twain was a pen name (a fake name he used when writing). The famous writer's real name was Samuel Langhorne Clemens. (His middle name is pronounced "Long Horn.") Fort Langhorn on Magic Kingdom's Tom Sawyer Island is named after him, even though it's spelled differently.

Hidden Mickey Alert (in the show)!

Look for the smoke cloud that forms after the fireworks burst behind the Statue of Liberty!

Want a real treat? If your parents happen to make dining reservations at Teppan Edo - a Japanese Steakhouse - your chef makes your meals right in front of you! It's a ton of fun, and one of the few places where a Cast Member actually "plays" with the food!

Kid's Tip!

Go to Restaurant Marrakesh in Morocco to see an actual letter from George Washington to the king of Morocco!

Take the time to explore the gardens and see all of the evergreen trees (trees that stay green year-round and don't lose their leaves) in the pavilion. Evergreen trees are special to the Japanese, because they symbolize eternal life.

The japanese word "Kawaii" means cute or loveable! Visit the Bijutsu-Kan Gallery

Did you know? The fountain in Italy is a replica of the famous *Trevi Fountain* in Rome. Visitors are told to toss a coin with their right hand over the left shoulder to guarantee they return someday. Try it to see if it works!

and see what all the rage is over cute things such as Hello Kitty. It's a Japanese pop-culture phenomenon anyone can get in on!

Did you know? Traditional trees found in Japan could not survive in the Florida climate, so Disney uses substitutes that look a lot like the authentic ones.

The American Adventure

Centered in World Showcase is the pavilion that represents The United States of America. By placing America in the middle, it serves as host to all the other countries of the world! In fact, the building in this pavilion is designed to look like arms stretched out to welcome the neighboring countries, and the setting is none other than Philadelphia, Pennsylvania, the city of brotherly love!

When you first enter the pavilion, you can explore the American Heritage Gallery - a collection of American art that changes every few months. Interactive displays will teach you more about the art, artifacts and history of the current art subject (such as from American Indian communities).

Did you know? The Grimm Brothers wrote the original Snow White story. The story influenced Walt Disney at a very early age. He became very *fond* of Germans and Germany. Dense European forests and snow-topped mountains like those found in Germany are a common natural setting for many of Walt's productions.

Hidden Mickey Alert!

Look at the grass in the miniature train village.

Independence Hall (similar to the real one in Philadelphia) holds an entertaining show called The American Adventure that celebrates the American spirit. This production tells the history of America in an educational and inspirational way. There are life-like Audio-Animatronic figures of some presidents, while Benjamin Franklin and Mark Twain narrate the story.

Did you know? You can meet princesses and characters in many of the lands within World Showcase. However, the princess in Germany is special. Snow White was the very first Disney princess!

The show honors heroes from history, tells of the Pilgrims, and gives honorable mentions to influences on American culture: Alexander Graham Bell, baseball great Jackie Robinson, Susan B. Anthony and even Walt Disney. We bet the proud ending gives you goosebumps!

The "robots" or Audio-Animatronics in the show look so real that you may forget they are elaborate machines. Ben Franklin appears to actually walk up stairs!

St. George and the Dragon

There is a large fountain in the center of the Germany pavilion courtyard. Fountains like this were common in German villages since the Middle Ages. Indoor plumbing wouldn't be available for centuries, and the fountain was the central water source for townsfolk to fill their water pails.

The fountain in the Germany pavilion is a monument to St. George and his victorious battle over a dragon. His tale goes back over a millennium (1,000 years!). Monuments to St. George, who is the Catholic patron saint of soldiers, are common throughout Bavaria, a German state.

Did you know? Look for the statue of Saint George on top of the pavilion's "water source." It isn't just a decoration. The saint is protecting the town's water to ensure good health for the village.

According to legend:

St. George was a Roman soldier and priest from the Middle East.

A poisonous dragon made its den within a city's water source. In order to draw water from the spring, citizens would bring the dragon an offering to distract it.

They started by bringing sheep, but those soon ran out. Then they offered young maidens who were misfortunate enough to be chosen by *drawing lots* (a type of unlucky lottery). When all the girls except for the king's daughter were gone, the king begged the dragon to spare her, but the dragon was greedy.

The king then called upon all knights of the land to battle the dragon. The winner would marry the beautiful princess.

St. George was determined to be her champion and set out to slay the dragon the following day.

As soon as the dragon saw him, it rushed from its cave, roaring louder than thunder. Its head was immense, and its tail was fifty feet long. But St. George was not afraid.

He struck the monster with his spear, hoping to wound it. The dragon's scales were so hard that the spear broke into a thousand pieces. The impact caused St. George to fall from his horse.

Fortunately, he rolled under an enchanted orange tree against where the dragon's venom could not affect him. Within a few minutes St. George had recovered his strength and was able to fight again.

He charged the beast with his sword, but the dragon spewed poison on him, causing his armor split in two.

Once more, St. George hid and refreshed himself from the orange tree.

Finally, with sword in hand, the brave knight rushed the dragon and pierced it under the wing, where there were no protective scales. Defeated, the dragon fell to his death at St. George's feet.

This story was a favorite among Christian crusaders who pushed militant Muslims out of Europe and brought the tale home to be retold again and again. A statue of St. George is also found in the Italy pavilion, and his bravery is celebrated with a holiday in the United Kingdom.

Italy

The Italy pavilion looks like the waterfront city of Venice. Look up at the "small" replica of the Campanile (the tall bell tower that soars above the pavilion). Gondolas (pronounced "gone-dolas") are tied up to the dock in the water. These small boats are used to move along the canals in Italy. (Unfortunately, the ones in the pavilion are just for show.)

In Italy, city hall bell towers replaced the church spires that commonly soared above other towns. Pedestrians (people traveling on foot) rule everything there.

The courtyard at the Italy pavilion is a place for you to leisurely stroll around the restaurants and shops. You can find a perfume shop, a place to buy handmade masks (for the prince's ball!) and even a gelato stand (a super-tasty Italian ice cream)!

Germany

The Germany pavilion combines elements from small and large towns all around Germany. As home to Disney's very first princess, Snow White, look for *Snow White's Wishing Well* where she meets guests!

Visit the giant cuckoo clock in the town square to hear it chime and see the characters run around. It runs for a couple minutes at the top of every hour (when the minute hand, or big hand, points at the 12 on the clock). Listen to the classical music from the glockenspiel (which is how the clock chimes).

You can buy a cuckoo clock of your own in one of the shops. There are also lots of toys and teddy bears for sale!

Biergarten is a restaurant in the Germany pavilion that has a unique theme. Even though it is indoors, it seems like an outdoor German town inside the restaurant! If you have time, take a couple of hours out of the day to eat dinner at this buffet restaurant.

A live musical band (called an "oompah band") plays authentic music on a stage. The musicians use many types of classic instruments, like bells, an accordion and guitars. They also have xylophones and an alpine horn, which is long and reaches to the ground. The band sings, yodels and dances on stage. There is even a big dance floor if you get in the mood to cut a rug! When you hear the tunes, it is hard to resist.

Did you know? It's normal to sit down and eat at a table with strangers in Germany. You might get seated "German-style" if you eat at the Biergarten restaurant!

Germany is known for its excellent sauerkraut, sausage and cheeses. What you really might like to try is some German chocolate! Be sure to check out the stores, too. There's a Christmas ornament store and a crystal shop with real princess tiaras. Let your nose guide you to the caramel shop, where all the sweets are made with the sticky treat!

As you leave Germany, take a walk along the Romantic Road. There's an entire miniature German village there, complete with a working train.

China

Visit the Temple of Heaven in the China pavilion. It is modeled after a temple in the Chinese city of Beijing. Inside is the incredible 360-degree Circle Vision theater that completely surrounds you! China's movie is called, Reflections of China and takes you on a tour of the beautiful scenery across the country. The theater is decorated in red and gold, which are good-luck colors.

While visiting China, be sure to have a look through its massive department store. Try a fruity can of soda with real bits of fruit inside. Yum!

Did you know? Lots of people miss one of the most interesting things in the China pavilion – an entire army made of stone!

These "Tomb Warriors" are replicas of a real stone army that was uncovered in China.

It is believed they were carved to protect members of royalty after death.

The original one that was discovered had over 8,000 soldiers, each one completely different!

Listen for the flute music playing in the courtyard. Enjoy the serene setting as you skip through garden paths. There are even koi ponds filled with goldfish to enjoy!

Kid's Tip!

Most of World Showcase opens at 11 am, but the Norway pavilion (including the Frozen Ever After ride) opens at the same time as Future World. Run straight for Frozen Ever After when the park opens if you don't have a Lightning Lane reservation for it.

Want a little more excitement? Watch out for live acrobats who perform daily in the courtyard. Mulan also makes daily appearances in the China pavilion. (Check those Times Guides if you don't want to miss them!)

Finally, check out the House of the Whispering Willows - a dedicated gallery featuring Disney's most recent resort: Shanghai Disney Resort. Discover drawings, photos and artwork depicting how Disney Imagineers wove the Chinese culture and architecture into this newest Disney Resort.

Norway

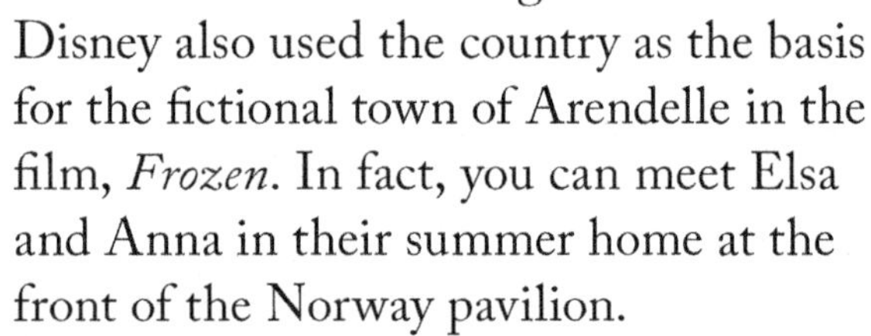

Norway has a very unique history and culture that includes trolls and vikings. Disney also used the country as the basis for the fictional town of Arendelle in the film, *Frozen*. In fact, you can meet Elsa and Anna in their summer home at the front of the Norway pavilion.

Did you know? There's a real town in Norway called Arendal. It was established back in the 16th century (that's the 1500s)!

Frozen Ever After

At the rear of the pavilion, take a boat ride on *Frozen Ever After*. You journey to the ice palace, where Elsa is waiting to greet visitors from all around the globe.

Of course, all of your friends, including Anna, Kristoff and Olaf, the friendly snowman, join you along the way. This is a really popular ride. If you don't get a Lightning Lane reservation for it, prepare to have a long wait!

Kid's Tip!

Get a Lightning Lane reservation for the boat ride in Norway: *Frozen Ever After*.

Near the front of the pavilion, you can visit the *Stave Church* gallery which tells the tale of ancient Norse Gods, such as Thor and Odin. The building looks a lot like a boat on its end, because that it is the type of construction the ancient Norwegians knew how to build. It is very solid against harsh weather.

Another really popular place is the *Akershus* restaurant, which has all your favorite princesses to meet while you eat! The restaurant gets its name and design from the real Akershus, an ancient castle that was once a fortress to protect the townsfolk in the capital city of Oslo.

Mexico

You can't miss the Mexico pavilion and its giant pyramid. The pyramid is similar to real ones found in Mexico. This one combines both Aztec and Mayan designs. These were ancient civilizations that used to live in Mexico.

Don't just admire it from the outside; inside the pyramid is a fun boat ride and an entire town center, complete with a restaurant and shops!

Celebrate Dia de Muertos (the Mexican holiday 'Day of the Dead') by viewing Mexican artwork at the Mexico Folk Art Gallery. You just might recognize some colorful artwork from Disney-Pixar's *Coco*!

Hidden Mickey Alert!

As the volcano at the back of the pyramid starts to erupt, the smoke swirls around in the form of Mickey!

Gran Fiesta Tour Starring the Three Caballeros

Gran Fiesta Tour Starring the Three Caballeros is the pavilion's boat ride. Three cartoon birds (Donald Duck, José and Panchito) are your hosts on the ride, and you follow them as they prepare to do a big show in Mexico City. The problem is that Donald keeps getting lost! (These three birds starred in a Disney cartoon that was released way back in 1944. That's over 70 years ago!)

You can meet Donald (and sometimes his friends) daily at a little meet-and-greet outside of the pyramid.

Did You Know? At the very tip-top of the pyramid is the control room for Epcot's evening fireworks show! That's right - all of the music, lights and pyrotechnics are controlled from this spot, as it gives a good view of the whole lagoon.

Entertainment

Pick up a Times Guide when you enter the park. It has a complete listing of any shows and entertainment happening that day. Most of the country pavilions in World Showcase have something neat to see (and a character to meet).

Look for performers throughout World Showcase. Some really fun ones include a rock band called British Revolution in the United Kingdom who put on a "jolly good show" (slang for fun!); the daring acrobats in China; the band of Japanese drummers; the Italian squad of flag performers; and live bands playing in The American Adventure (during festivals).

Harmonious

Every night at closing time is a huge fireworks show with flames (called pyrotechnics), lazers and awesome music. As classic Disney music booms over the loudspeakers, the crow learns how music inspires people.

The show takes place in the middle of World Showcase Lagoon, and you can see it from anywhere around the *lagoon*. (A lagoon is a small lake - sometimes manmade.)

About the Show

All of the action is controlled in a booth above the Mexico pavilion's pyramid, while on-site assistants closer to the lagoon keep an eye out for issues.

While waiting for the show, look for the 19 torches around World Showcase Lagoon. Each one represents one century (100 years) over the last two millennia (thousand-year period). The 20th torch, representing the 20th century, used to be the Unity Torch that was revealed during the former Epcot nighttime show.

If you like fireworks, you won't be disappointed. This isn't just a fireworks show, though.

Full-color laser systems shine from three locations around the lagoon: the American Adventure, Canada and Mexico pavilions. Projectors launch laser light as beams, scan patterns and images. ("Laser" is an acronym for "Light Amplification by Stimulated Emission of Radiation.)

Bounce mirrors are also scattered around the park on various islands and rooftops to further blanket the park in laser light. Overcast nights and evenings where the smoke from the fireworks lingers above the lagoon create an even more spectacular laser effect, as the light patterns reflect on the smoke clouds above the water.

Dancing water further illustrates the magic and inspiration of music. Watch the lagoon become a water wonderland!

It is a spectacular show and a perfect way to end your day at Epcot.

Kid's Tip!

You can see the Harmonious show really well from England, Canada or Mexico.

Water Fun

Outside the Imagination Pavilion, look for the jumping fountain - it's as if it's playing "leap frog" over the sidewalk!

There is another fun fountain near *Mission: SPACE.*

Bring a swimsuit under your clothes for the small water play areas in World Discovery.

Duck Tales World Showcase Adventure

Have you ever wanted to travel the world on a daring adventure? Here's your opportunity to help the Duck family fight villains and save the world!

You and your family can play an interactive game based on the hit Disney Channel cartoon, Duck Tales.

Ask your mom or dad to use their cell phone or tablet to download the Play Disney Parks app and sign up for this exciting adventure. The game will be available for play only when you get to World Showcase in Epcot.

Your adventure begins as you search for clues throughout World Showcase.

There are missions available in six pavilions: China, France, Germany, Japan, Mexico and United Kingdom. It doesn't cost anything extra to play the game, so once you complete one adventure, sign up for another!

Kids love playing this game with grown ups, but tell them to let you lead the way and control the smart device!

Kid's Tip!

There's a cool overhead view of Epcot if you take the monorail to the park. The train soars over a large portion of Future World, gliding about 20 feet above the walking paths.

JAMMitors

These musical entertainers have a loud and fun music show in World Celebration. Get your groove on while they bang out rhythms using garbage cans!

Pin Trading

You can trade Disney pins with other guests or Cast Members throughout Walt Disney World, but one of the best places to trade is in Epcot's World Celebration. Take a couple of pins with you when you visit a park in case you want to make a trade!

Make sure an adult is with you when you talk to anyone you don't know! Get permission for the pins you want to trade in case one of them is special to your parent or to your brother or sister!

Films

Of the films in The American Experience, Canada, France and China, pick just one or two. It is hard to see them all! But don't miss the rides in France, Norway and Mexico.

Character Meet & Greets

Get your autograph book ready!

You can collect autographs and pose for pictures with famous Disney characters throughout Epcot.

Mickey, Minnie, Goofy, and other classic characters can often be found throughout the day in World Celebration. Look for **Baymax** (*Big Hero 6*), **Joy** and **Sadness** (*Inside Out*) at one of the outdoor lawns in World Nature.

Many Disney princesses also appear around World Showcase, including Disney's very first princess from the animated film, *Snow White*. **Snow** can be found in the Germany pavilion, next to her wishing well.

Planning Your Day

Look for the Electronic Tip Board Signs with attraction wait times. Epcot has these located in the center of Innoventions Plaza in Epcot and near Test Track in World Discovery. You can also find these same wait times on your mobile device using the My Disney Experience app.

If you don't have an Individual Lightning Lane reservation for Frozen Ever After or Remy's Ratatouille Adventure, race to either of those rides as soon as the park opens. Next, head for Test Track, which is extremely popular. Head over to Soarin' after that. Check out The Seas with Nemo and Friends after you come out of The Land Pavilion. Then, if there's time, check out the Imagination pavilion.

Wait until mid-afternoon for Spaceship Earth and later in the evening for Mission: SPACE if you don't have Lightning Lane reservations for these rides. Of course, any Lightning Lane reservations will change the order of how you tour the neighborhoods of Epcot.

When the sun starts to beat down, take a cooling break inside Club Cool. Don't forget to rest every once in a while and keep drinking plenty of water! Look for counter-service restaurants indoors, such as Sunshine Seasons in The Land pavilion or Les Halles Boulangerie-Patisserie in the France pavilion to cool down and grab a quick bite to eat.

World Showcase opens two hours after the other Epcot neighborhoods (just in time for lunch). Get there right when it opens, and there are short lines for the shows.

TOP ATTRACTION RATINGS		
Super Cool (MUST-SEE)	**Cool (SHOULD SEE)**	**Fun (SEE IF YOU CAN)**
Frozen Ever After	Journey into Imagination with Figment	Living with the Land
Guardians of the Galaxy: Cosmic Rewind	Disney & Pixar Short Film Festival	Innoventions
Harmonious	Gran Fiesta Tour (Mexico)	The American Adventure – Educational and Patriotic Show!
Journey of Water, Inspired by Moana	Beauty & the Beast Film	Canada: Far and Wide
Mission: SPACE		Impressions de France
Remy's Ratatouille Adventure		Reflections of China
Soarin' Around the World		
Spaceship Earth		
Test Track		
The Seas with Nemo and Friends		
Every Country Pavilion!		

Epcot Favorites

Across

4. Where can you find a pyramid in World Showcase?

6. Can you imagine a dragon like him?

7. This ride will have you ________' high above the most famous places in the world.

8. This little rat will take you on an adventure through the streets of Paris.

10. Epcot's park icon is a geodesic __________.

Down

1. The __________ Adventure is the host pavilion for World Showcase.

2. Find a Beauty & The Beast ________ in the France Pavilion during the annual Flower & Garden Festival.

3. Create your own vehicle in a lab before setting out on this high speed ride.

5. Can you help Marlin and Dory find this little clownfish?

9. Queen _________ cordially invites you to her ice palace in Arendelle.

*Answers on Page 212

Let's Go to Hollywood Studios!

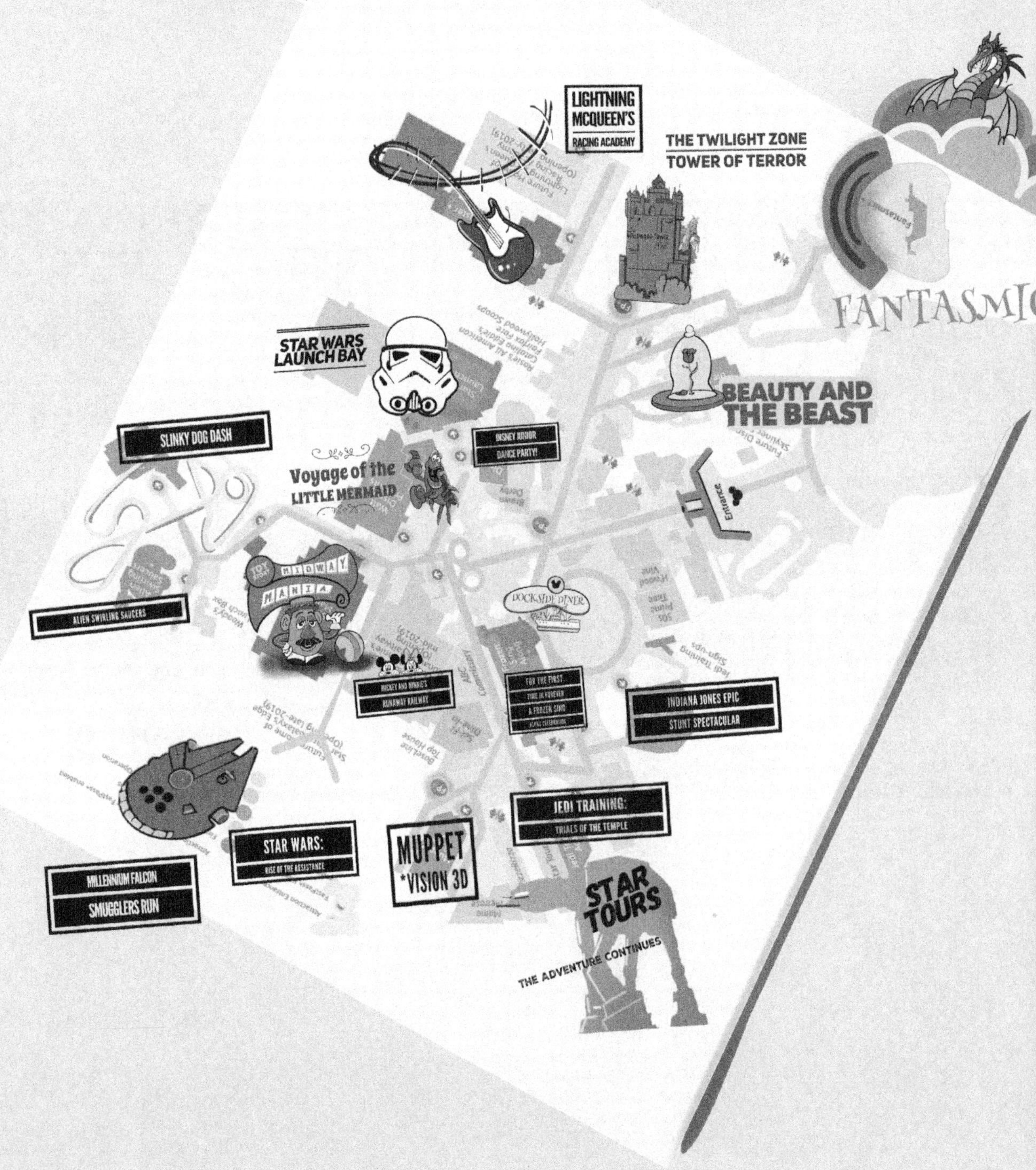

Highlights

The immersive *Toy Story and Star Wars: Galaxy's Edge Lands* are waiting for you to explore!

Take a spooky elevator ride on the *Tower of Terror.*

Go upside-down on the *Rock 'n' Roller Coaster*!

Battle the Dark Force at *Jedi Training: Trials of the Temple.*

Take a silly spin with Mickey & Minnie on the first and only ride to feature everyone's favorite mice: *Mickey & Minnie's Runaway Railway*!

Lights! Camera! Action!

Do you love *Toy Story*? Have you always wanted to be a Jedi? Hollywood Studios will take you into your favorite shows and make you part of the adventure! Become a Hollywood "big screen" legend, watch wild stunts, learn how they are performed and understand the magic of movie-making.

Hollywood Studios was given its name because real TV shows and movies used to be filmed there. The studios and backlot were taken out to make room for the park's most popular lands: *Toy Story Land* and *Star Wars: Galaxy's Edge.*

One section of Hollywood Studios looks just like the city of Hollywood did back in its heyday (that means its prime years), when movies became really popular in the 1930s and 1940s.

Some of your favorite shows represented at this park include *Indiana Jones, Star Wars, Frozen, The Little Mermaid, The Muppets* and *Toy Story.*

If you like wild rides, this park has two of the best: Rock 'n' Roller Coaster, which turns you upside down, and *Tower of Terror,* the spookiest elevator ride in the world!

Since Hollywood Studios is all about entertainment, the shows can't be beat; there are two evening shows with fireworks! There are also some of the most unique characters to meet, including Olaf from *Frozen*, as well as Chewbacca and BB-8 from *Star Wars*!

Attractions

Mickey & Minnie's Runaway Railway

Get ready for some silly fun when you board your train. Goofy is your conductor on this zany, action-packed ride.

When things go wrong, Mickey and Minnie race to save you. During your journey, dodge obstacles through twists and turns, and take a dance lesson with Daisy — all in your wild, trackless vehicle!

The Twilight Zone Tower of Terror

Inside of the 199-foot high Hollywood Tower Hotel is the tallest ride at Walt Disney World. The Tower of Terror takes you on a scary trip in an elevator where you drop down and propel up at super-fast speeds.

Did You Know? The Federal Aviation Administration (FAA) *regulates* aircraft. They require any building 200 feet (20 stories!) high or taller to have a blinking red light on top of it. That's to warn any low flying aircraft. Because of this, Disney built the Tower of Terror (as well as Cinderella Castle and Expedition Everest) as tall as they could without being required by law to install a red, blinking light - because red lights would take away from their special theming!

As you walk through, take a look around at all the stuff left behind when the hotel's last guests abandoned it many years ago.

After the lobby, you enter one of two libraries on either side. Look around the shelves at the interesting knick-knacks. Things can get a bit scary as the lights suddenly turn off and a black and white TV turns on, but it's all part of the story.

Rod Serling, the host from a 1960s black and white TV show called *The Twilight Zone,* comes on the TV. He tells visitors about the legend of the hotel.

The doors open and you're on your way into the furnace boiler room in the basement. Inside this room are the hotel's four service elevators. When the doors open, you are ushered into an elevator-like car.

Buckle your seat belt for a bumpy ride!

The first part of the ride is a short tour of the hotel where you get a glimpse of the ghosts that disappeared. Are they beckoning you to join them?

Did you know? Tall buildings in the United States don't usually have a 13th floor. This is based on the superstition that 13 is an unlucky number. Take a look at the floor buttons in the elevator next time you're in one of these buildings. The floors skip from 12 to 14!

Your elevator car travels into another, pitch-black elevator shaft. Hold onto your hat as the elevator cable snaps and you drop several floors before coming to an abrupt stop. After it falls, the car reverses direction and you are swept back up the

Kid's Tip!

If you do brave the Tower of Terror, make sure anything loose is secured. You don't want your change or snacks to fly around the car.

A Spooky Fun History!

The Twilight Zone Tower of Terror has its own scary backstory:

Back in the 1930s, The Hollywood Tower Hotel was a popular hotel for Hollywood's hottest stars.

On Halloween night in 1939, the regular hotel elevators were out of order, so only the service elevators were in use. One very notable group of guests took the maintenance elevator up after checking in at the lobby: Sally Shine, a child star; Emmeline Partridge, Sally's nanny; Caroline Crosson, a rising Hollywood starlette; Gilbert London, one of Caroline's admirers; and Dewey Todd, Jr., bellhop and son of the hotel's builder.

Lightning struck the elevator with the group in it, causing it to plummet and crash at the bottom. The bodies were removed secretly, and the Dewey's distraught father closed the hotel.

The hotel was abandoned that fateful night and is now said to be haunted by their spirits.Nobody has set foot there for about 80 years, so the hotel lobby is exactly as guests left it -- with the addition of lots of cobwebs and dust!

elevator shaft - sometimes all the way to the top - as quickly as you dropped!

Did you know? There's a plaque on the elevator that says it was last serviced with a number of 10259. This references the date the very first episode of The Twilight Zone aired on October 2, 1959. Notice that Mr. Cadwallader was the employee to check it. That's the name of a creepy character from "Escape Clause," the sixth episode of the show's first season.

You get to take several, blazing-fast trips up and down the hotel elevator shaft.

One trip to the 13th floor pauses just long enough to snap your picture. (Be sure to look for your souvenir photo after the ride!)

For many kids, this is the scariest ride they have ever been on. If you can make it past your fear, the thrill is totally worth it!

Did You Know? There is actually a 5th elevator available; it's often called the "chicken elevator."

If you make it through the boiler room and decide you don't want to ride, you can ask to take the "chicken exit" (or elevator).

A Cast Member will allow you to board a normal elevator which will deposit you safely near the gift shop where others exit the ride. Try to be brave, though. We promise it's more fun than scary!

Handles are located in front of the seats if you need something to hold onto (other than Mom or Dad), but it's way more fun to throw your hands in the air!

When you finish this ride, look for your photo in the PhotoPass area. There can be some really funny expressions on people's faces, especially yours!

Minimum Height Required:
40" tall (3 feet, 4 inches)

Rock 'n' Roller Coaster

Get ready to rock-and-roll on your high-speed journey to a concert. Hop into your super-stretch limousine for the wild ride. (It's really a long roller coaster car that looks like a limousine!)

Hop in and wait for the light to turn green; the countdown begins… 3….2….1… GO! Hold onto your Mickey ears! At the beginning of the roller coaster ride, you take off from zero and reach the top speed of 60 miles an hour in a matter of just three seconds!

The coaster then quickly loops around three inversions (that means you go upside down!) as you are whisked on your stretch limousine down a California highway.

Did you know? Each stretch limousine has a license plate on the back. The plate number is a secret code that identifies which song(s) will play during your wild ride.

Kid's Tip!

There's a special pocket for loose stuff (hats and sunglasses) in your car. Use it, so you don't lose something on this ride!

The limousine's radio is tuned to a live rock and roll concert; You get to listen to music all the way!

The ride ends when you arrive at the concert venue. When you exit, you get to walk the red carpet and see the concert being performed live on a big screen.

This is Disney's fastest roller coaster and the only one with inversions. Kids love it!

Minimum Height Required:
48" tall (4 feet)

Lightning McQueen's Racing Academy

Calling all future race car drivers (and anyone who just loves fun)! The one-and-only Lightning McQueen has agreed to teach you the ins and outs of what it's like to be a race car.

Get ready to laugh until your sides hurt in this silly and fun show.

Beauty and the Beast – Live on Stage

Sing along to the musical stage show that tells the story of Belle and the Beast's adventure and how they fell in love.

The story follows Disney's animated film, though this stage show moves much faster than the movie (removing some scenes to shorten it into a

30-minute show). This may be a bit difficult to follow along if you've never seen the movie, so make sure you watch it before you go to Walt Disney World!

At the beginning of the story, Belle is tired of her small-town life. She dreams of what it would be like to live an exciting, adventurous life away from her small village.

While searching for her father who has disappeared, Belle becomes prisoner in Beast's castle. She discovers enchanted characters there, including Lumiere, Cogsworth, Mrs. Potts and others. They were put under a magic spell that turned them into household items.

As time goes on, Belle and her enchanted friends help Beast discover he is a good person deep inside and can come to care for others. Be there when the curse is broken and Beast and the others turn back into their human forms.

Everyone enjoys the bright colors, dancing and music, especially singing along to "Be Our Guest!"

There are several performances each day. Check the Times Guide (that you can pick up at the entrance to each park and at most shops) for the daily schedule.

*Muppet*Vision 3D*

The Muppets put on one of the funnest shows for kids of all ages. Even your parents and grandparents will have a laugh during this show!

Enjoy the pre-show in the lobby that's full of silly props and jokes. Fozzy the Bear, Gonzo, Scooter and Sam Eagle entertain you on TVs mounted above the room.

When you enter the theater, it should look familiar. It's exactly like the one you see on Jim Henson's The Muppet Show.

Put on your 3D glasses to enjoy tons of special effects during the big screen show and Audio-Animatronic (mechanical) effects in the theater. There are things going on in all directions, and some of the best action is taking place in the theater itself.

The effects are so amazing, it's hard to tell what is real and what's on the screen. It looks like you could reach out and touch what's not really there! Miss Piggy's big singing routine brings with it bubbles that appear to rain down on the audience! (Or are they real bubbles?!)

Look for the Swedish Chef cooking up a dish in the back of the theater! As if things couldn't get better, the real, live Sweetums makes an appearance near the end of the show!

This is a great show and highly recommended. Be sure to add it to your list of attractions to see at Disney's Hollywood Studios!

Star Wars Launch Bay

Do you love Star Wars? This building is home to some really awesome Star Wars things. Real and replica memorabilia from the movies are on display. You can even meet some of the characters. Be sure to get photos of everything, including the Cantina!

Explore every inch of the building. There's a special area with video games you can play!

Star Tours – The Adventures Continue

This is a fun, 3D motion-simulated attraction that lets you fly through galaxies far, far away! You are in a spaceship rocketing through different Star Wars scenes on a mad dash to escape Darth Vader and the Dark Side.

The flight simulator has about 50 different scenarios, so each journey is vastly different and a complete surprise. C-3PO pilots your ship, and you may encounter many of your favorite characters, such as Princess Leia, Yoda, R2-D2 and even Darth Vader!

This is a bumpy ride that shakes you around. The wild ride has sharp turns and quick drops that seem very, very real.

Like all simulated attractions, don't eat anything before you board! If you begin to feel sick during the ride, close your eyes and it will get a bit better.

Minimum Height Required: 40" tall (3 feet, 4 inches)

Jedi Training: Trials of the Temple

May the Force be with you!

Don't just watch the action, become part of it! Kids between 4 and 12 can become a Junior Jedi (called a *Padawan*) and fight the Dark Side of the Force. Your family and friends will watch *You* in the show!

Kid's Tip!

Try not to sign up for mid-afternoon shows on super hot days. You are going to be outside for about an hour, which can be really uncomfortable! If you can, get a spot in an early morning or evening show if you plan to stay in the park all day.

Train with a Master Jedi to learn the skills needed to defeat Darth Vader and the Seventh Sister during your Padawan training. Padawans are issued a real Jedi robe and a training lightsaber (just to borrow, not to keep) and are taught the ways of the Force.

Become a part of the show and get onstage by signing up at the Indiana Jones Adventure Outpost, near the Star Tours attraction.

Kid's Tip!

If you really want to do the jedi training, race to sign up first thing in the morning. It's the only way to make sure you get a spot in a show. Lots of kids want to do this. Space is very limited!

Even if you don't become part of the show, you can still watch the other kids battle the Dark Side. Don't miss it!

Millennium Falcon: Smugglers Run

Become a pilot, gunner or engineer, as you take a wild motion-simulated ride in the Millennium Falcon (Han Solo's spaceship from the *Star Wars* movies)!

Your mission is to retrieve supplies, but can you make it out with the ship in one piece?

Each ride is a bit unique, since you actually have some control over the ship's movements!

Minimum Height Required:
38" tall (3 feet, 2 inches)

Kid's Tip!

There's a secret "Chewie Mode" you can unlock on the *Millennium Falcon: Smugglers Run* attraction. Do a web search before your trip to find out how to do this special experience.

Star Wars: Rise of the Resistance

Are you ready to join the resistance? Expect trouble during your first mission when a First Order Star Destroyer captures your transport.

Prepare to battle your way to freedom on this one-of-a-kind, multi-platform ride.

Minimum Height Required:
40" tall (3 feet, 4 inches)

For the First Time in Forever: A Frozen Sing-Along Celebration

If you still can't get enough *Frozen*, you can join the singing fun at this storytelling and sing-along experience!

This fun and interactive show takes place in Arendelle, where the new

historians retell the *Frozen* story. They get the audience singing as film clips are shown on giant screens.

Sing-along to the fun songs of *Frozen*, including the all-time crowd favorite, Let it Go! Don't worry if you don't know all the words. They are shown on the screens as the songs play, along with a bouncing snowflake that helps you keep up.

Your favorites join in on the fun, including Elsa, Anna and Kristoff too!

Kid's Tip!

If you don't have a Lightning Lane reservation, show up early to get good seats.

Vacation Fun - An Original Animated Short with Mickey & Minnie

Head to the Mickey Shorts Theater near Echo Lake and enjoy watching Mickey and Minnie celebrate their favorite vacation memories.

Cool off inside this air-conditioned theater and be entertained by Mickey himself! After the show, pose with your family among some life-size recreations from Mickey's world!

Walt Disney Presents

This attraction helps you learn more about Walt's life. Find out how he and his brother started The Walt Disney Company. He also revolutionized the art of *animation* (cartoons).

It is a self-paced, walk-through museum containing displays that let you learn about the story of Walt and Roy Disney and how they created the magic.

Parents and grandparents love to take their time strolling through this museum. Don't rush them!

Did you know? Mickey Mouse was not Walt Disney's first cartoon character. Oswald the Lucky Rabbit came first.

The company Walt worked for owned the rights to use the character, so Walt had to create a new one. Oswald looks like he could be Mickey's longer-eared brother!

Everyone knows Mickey Mouse, his girlfriend Minnie and his puppy, Pluto. Walt created them in 1928 - that's more than 90 years ago! But did you know Mickey was originally going to be called Mortimer Mouse? Thankfully, Walt's wife, Lillian told him "Mickey" was a better name!

Many of Walt's personal belongings are on display in this museum. Look for old family photos, his piano, the first Audio-Animatronic figure (President Abraham Lincoln), and even the Academy Award Disney won for the first full-length motion picture (cartoon), *Snow White and the Seven Dwarfs.*

As you explore, discover plans for new and exciting things at the Disney parks, including brand-new attractions that will soon open!

Take your time to explore the exhibits. Then, watch a short film in a theater attached to the museum.

Kid's Tip!

Ask the Cast Member at the *Walt Disney Presents* entrance for a Citizenship Test.

If you answer all the questions correctly, you can sign your name in the citizenship book! Everyone wants to become a "Citizen of Walt Disney World!"

Indiana Jones Epic Stunt Spectacular

The *Indiana Jones Epic Stunt Spectacular* is a real, live movie set that teaches how certain scenes from Raiders of the Lost Ark were filmed and made using special effects! It gets really loud with fire and explosives to show how special effects are performed - but it's all controlled! If you think you may be startled by the noise of gunshots or explosions, sit towards the back and bring along earplugs.

Kid's Tip!

Look for the sign outside and to the left of the Indiana Jones entrance that says "Do not pull the rope." ("Not" is crossed out, so it looks like it says "Pull the rope!")

At the bottom of a well, an archaeologist is searching for precious artifacts at a dig site. Listen for sounds of digging.

Sometimes he drops something when the rope is pulled!

Kid's Tips!

- You can get into the park just before the official opening time to start your visit early. Go to Star Wars: Rise of the Resistance immediately. Then race to Slinky Dog Dash and Rock 'n' Roller Coaster first thing if you don't have Lightning Lane reservations. They get busy right away.
- Exits are available at the end of the line for Tower of Terror and Rock 'n' Roller Coaster if you get cold feet and decide to skip the ride at the last minute. These are called "chicken exits." Don't worry if you change your mind. Many adults freak out, too!
- Don't eat for at least an hour before going on any extreme ride, real or simulated. They can make you get sick. At Hollywood Studio, these are Rock 'n' Roller Coaster, Star Tours,Twilight Zone Tower of Terror and Millennium Falcon: Smugglers Run.
- Some of the stage shows don't start until later in the morning. Check your Times Guide.
- If you sit in the front rows at Fantasmic, you are likely to get wet! Select seats in the middle of the theater for the best place to see the show.

Kid's Tip!

Get to Indiana Jones at least 15 minutes before the show starts. Some adults get selected from the audience to take part alongside the professional stunt performers.

It's not safe for kids to join in, but you can still raise your hand and point out a parent to participate!

The action is fast and exciting. The show begins with a giant boulder rolling down that crushes the stuntman playing Indiana Jones... or does it? Learn exactly how the stuntman is kept perfectly safe during this scene, even though it appears he's getting squashed! Later on, an out-of-control airplane nearly does Indy in.

The stunt men and women make everything look easy, but it takes a lot of hard work! Observe all the "behind the scenes" tricks that happen to make a movie appear real and dangerous, when in reality, it's all performed with movie magic!

Toy Story Mania!

Shrink down to the size of a toy and help test out of all Andy's new shooting gallery games. This ride is a real blast!

If you read about Buzz Lightyear's Spin in the Magic Kingdom and thought it sounded cool, this ride is even more awesome! What makes it different is that it's 4-D (so you wear special glasses).

Your ride vehicle spins into colorful rooms full of special effects and fun targets to shoot at. Pull the trigger on your blaster to "shoot" balls, darts, rings and other fun toys at the targets!

Your car holds four people (two on each side) and has an electronic scorecard that keeps track of your fancy shooting. Compete with others to see who can rack up the most points.

Throughout the ride, try to spot all your favorite *Toy Story* characters, including Buzz, Woody, Jessie, Rex and Hamm. They cheer you on!

This is a fun game for kids of all ages - it's even a favorite among Grandparents!

Kid's Tip!

Kids love to go on Toy Story Midway Mania again and again. Show up early and you might be able to get on it a couple of times before the line gets too long. If you play it enough, you just might figure out hidden ways to score more points!

Since it's one of the few attractions for any age at Hollywood Studios, it's very popular. Get Lightning Lane reservations or visit early in the day to avoid waiting too long.

Kid's Tip!

If you're not sure about Rock 'n' Roller Coaster, ride Slinky Dog Dash first. It's the perfect starter coaster to prepare you for the big kid rides!

Slinky Dog Dash

This is a super fun roller coaster made just for kids. It's so fun, even adults love it!

Slinky Dog Dash takes you on a wild ride across Andy's backyard inside of the lovable Toy Story character.

Your coaster car is inside of his slinky coils, which twist, turn and zip around corners.

Minimum Height Required:
38" tall (3 feet, 2 inches)

Alien Swirling Saucers

Get ready to go for a spin! Andy won a new toy at Pizza Planet that features those little, green aliens.

Hold on to your hat, while you spin through space. Will you be lucky enough to be chosen by "The Claw"?

This isn't really a crazy spin ride like the *Mad Tea Party* in Magic Kingdom, so it shouldn't make you very dizzy. It's just great fun to get pulled along and twirl behind the little green aliens!

Minimum Height Required:
32" tall (2 feet, 8 inches)

Entertainment

Fantasmic!

The best way to end a day at Hollywood Studios is to view the nightly fireworks spectacular starring Mickey Mouse in his biggest role of all time!

Fantasmic! is an entertaining show containing fun, technical elements such as water, lasers and lights, and of course, famous Disney characters!

This show is set to a music soundtrack that every kid enjoys, your parents will remember many of these songs from when they were kids!

As the show begins, we enter Mickey's dream world. Disney villains show up to turn his dreams into nightmares. But don't worry too much, good always defeats evil, turning his dreams happy again!

This is a very popular show! The line starts forming at least an hour before the show begins.

If you arrive late, you might not get a good seat. On busy days, you might not get into the show at all!

This incredible blend of live action, video, water ballet and fireworks show plays most evenings, often twice when the park is open late.

Kid's Tip!

If *Fantasmic!* is playing twice on the day you visit, go to the later show. It's usually much less crowded and easier to find a good seat.

The show is about 30 minutes long and is held in the Hollywood Hills Amphitheater. This outdoor theater uses metal stadium bleachers, and the evening performances can get very chilly (except in summer).

The main stage is surrounded by a water moat for the floating parade of characters. Certain parts of the show have pyrotechnics, so you might feel the heat from those displays (and get a little wet) if you sit close to the stage!

Scenes from Fantasia, Cinderella, Mulan, Pinocchio, Dumbo, and many others appear before the audience on screens that are made out of water! In-between these aquatic screen scenes, live-action scenes take place that include your favorite Disney characters and villains.

Watch a battle scene from Pocahontas, see the Disney Princess and Princes float by on boats, hear the Evil Queen cast her spooky spell, and watch out for the Maleficent dragon to make an appearance! In Disney-like fashion, Mickey has some magic up his sleeve to end this nightmare once and for all!

Kid's Tip!

Fantasmic! is located in the outdoor theater next to the Tower of Terror. It is right next to a lake, so if you take a boat ride between Hollywood Studios and Epcot at night, you can hear the show going on.

A crowd-pleasing finale including Steamboat Willie and all his friends ends the show, along with fun fireworks!

Star Wars: A Galactic Spectacular

Light and Dark clash in an incredible display of lasers, lights, fireworks and movie scenes. Watch as the Force is brought to life and clips from your favorite Star Wars movies play out using the Chinese Theater as a screen.

As the powers collide, lasers and fireworks shoot across the sky.

This is one of the most powerful and immersive shows Walt Disney World has to offer. Don't miss it!

Kid's Tip!

Find a place to stand and watch the show very early. Look for somewhere in the courtyard in front of the theater, but not too close to the building. The streets fill up quickly for this performance every night.

Character Meet & Greets

There are a lot of places to meet characters at Disney's Hollywood Studios.

The Incredibles greet kids on Pixar Place, while Mickey and Minnie have a special location on the Red Carpet, just off of Commissary Lane. Nearby, Olaf is always celebrating summer near Echo Lake.

Chewbacca, **Kylo Ren** and **BB-8**, everyone's favorite droid, can be found in *Star Wars Launch Bay*. Just outside, meet **Disney Junior Pals** in the *Animation Courtyard*.

Meanwhile, **Buzz Lightyear**, **Woody** and their friends are on-hand to greet kids in the spectacular *Toy Story Land*.

Be sure to ask a Cast Member for a Guide Map and Times Guide to see who is there the day you visit.

TOP ATTRACTION RATINGS		
Super Cool (MUST-SEE)	**Cool (SHOULD SEE)**	**Fun (SEE IF YOU CAN)**
Toy Story Mania!	Disney Junior Dance Party!	Walt Disney Presents
Slinky Dog Dash	Beauty and the Beast – Live on Stage	
The Twilight Zone Tower of Terror	Alien Swirling Saucers	
Rock 'n' Roller Coaster	Muppet Vision 3-D	
Mickey & Minnie's Runaway Railway	Millennium Falcon: Smugglers Run	
Indiana Jones Epic Stunt Spectacular		
Lightning McQueen's Racing Academy		
Fantasmic!		
Star Wars: Rise of the Resistance		
Star Tours - The Adventures Continue		
Star Wars: A Galactic Spectacular		

Hollywood Studios Favorites

Across

3. ________ Dog Dash takes you on a wild ride through Andy's backyard.
5. Learn how to race from Lightning ________.
7. Battle Darth ________ in the Jedi Training Academy.
9. Try to get passes to see this band at Rock 'n' Rollercoaster.
10. First name of the adventurer who shows you an "Epic Stunt Spectacular."

Down

1. Mickey and ________ finally got their first theme park ride in Hollywood Studios.
2. Go on a high speed adventure in the famous Millennium ________.
4. The Tower of ________ is Walt Disney World's spookiest park icon.
6. These little aliens take you on a spin, hoping to be chosen by "The ________."
8. Hollywood Studios used to be a working movie and television ________.

*Answers on Page 212

Let's Go to Animal Kingdom!

Bring out your wild side!

Disney's Animal Kingdom is a celebration of nature and many kinds of animals. You get to discover African lions, Asian tigers, Zebras, Giant tortoises (a kind of turtle) and many more. There are even creatures from another planet!

> **Did you know?** Giant tortoises have been around since the time of the dinosaurs!

As you know, dinosaurs were a type of animal, and there's an entire land devoted to the behemoths in the Animal Kingdom. (Behemoth means gigantic!)

Thrills await with wild attractions, including a spooky roller coaster ride in Yeti territory, a real safari through Africa, a zany adventure to the Dinosaur age and an out-of-this-world experience on the back of a Banshee!

Like the Magic Kingdom, the Animal Kingdom is separated into different lands:

Discovery Island

Dinoland U.S.A.

Asia

Africa

Pandora

Oasis

Enter through an area called The Oasis. (An oasis is a place where water and plants exist in an otherwise dry area, like a desert.) The Animal Kingdom's Oasis is filled with greenery, birds and animals in natural environments.

> **Did you know?** The park is actually sunk into the ground to make it cooler and more comfortable for the animals.

Asia Highlights

Get soaked on Kali River Rapids!

Face the monstrous Yeti on a runaway train with Expedition Everest.

Africa Highlights

Go on a real safari and see live animals with Kilimanjaro Safaris.

Explore Rafiki's Planet Watch.

See The Lion King roar in a musical extravaganza.

DinoLand Highlights (Closing Later in 2023)

Go back in time and encounter dinos on DINOSAUR.

Become an archaeologist at The Boneyard playground.

Pandora Highlights

Soar the skies on a banshee in Pandora: Flight of Passage.

Here the shaman sing on Na'vi River Journey.

> **Did you know?** All the real animals at Animal Kingdom came from special parks and zoos around the world. None of them were taken from nature. They are all treated very, very well, and given lots to eat and plenty of time to play. In fact, Disney created such realistic animal habitats that many zoos copied their methods!

Attractions

Discovery Island

Discovery Island serves as the gateway to the other lands (just like the "hub" at the Magic Kingdom).

Be sure to check out the gigantic *Tree of Life*. Its massive branches hover 145 feet high, right in the center of Discovery Island (which is at the center of the entire park).

Hidden Mickey Alert!

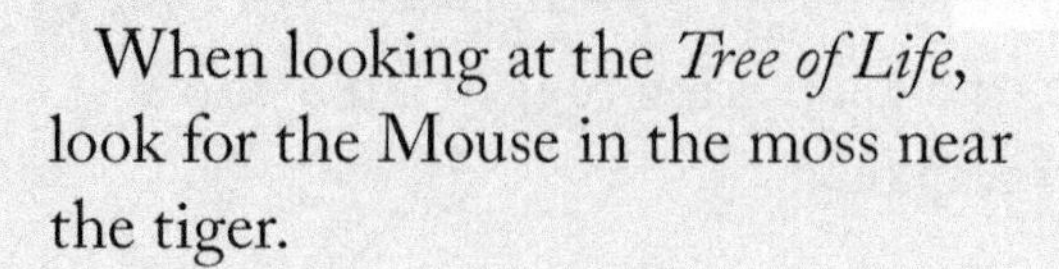

When looking at the *Tree of Life*, look for the Mouse in the moss near the tiger.

It's Tough to Be a Bug!

A huge theater is located underneath the Tree of Life. You can sit down and watch a show based on the classic Disney film, A Bug's Life. It's a 4-D experience, meaning you watch a 3-D film using special glasses while special effects, such as smells, water and Audio-Animatronic characters make it even more realistic.

Did you know? *It's Tough to Be a Bug* was released before *A Bug's Life* opened in theaters.

Flik, the ant, hosts the show. He wants to tell you all about the humongous number of little creatures that inhabit our planet. Things get a little scary when Flik's enemy, Hopper the Grasshopper, arrives with some eight-legged friends.

Because the theater is underground, the temperature is always pretty cool (which feels great if you visit on a hot day). The theater is spacious and dark, just like how you would expect an underground cavern to be.

Did you know? The *Tree of Life* is not a real tree at all. Though it looks ordinary from a distance, as you get up close, you realize that there is nothing ordinary about it at all. It is an extravagant work of art.

Within the bark and roots are hundreds of animal carvings. Artists designed it with 325 animals in all! Some of the really big ones are easy to see, while others take a little more searching.

There are over 8,000 branches that hold over 102,000 leaves! Each leaf is man-made - again, nothing 'natural' about them, although they look very real! Recently, each leaf was replaced with a new leaf that contains LED lighting effects. This helps enhance the nighttime effect, including special effects for *Tree of Life Awakenings*.

It also took a tremendous effort to build the huge structure. (It is actually built on the frame of an offshore oil derrick!)

Creepy Crawlies

Some kids get scared because of the creepy crawlies in the dark environment. If you don't like insects and bugs, you may find this show too extreme. Watch out for the giant animatronic spiders!

Kid's Tip!

Close your eyes if you get too spooked. The scary part ends quickly!

Kid's Tip!

Sit back and straight up against your chair to make sure you don't miss the surprise ending of *It's Tough to Be a Bug*!

Wilderness Explorers

The wilderness must be explored! And you can do just that in this exclusive (and free) club that's just for kids! Join Russell, from the *UP!* movie, and earn badges from educational stations located all throughout the Animal Kingdom park!

The headquarters to join Wilderness Explorers is located near the front of the park, on your way to the giant tree at the end of the road. Stop at the booth, take the official pledge, and receive your free guide book that gives you missions to complete and earn badges.

As you visit each station, encounter a variety of challenges and learning opportunities. It's so much fun! Don't worry. If you get stumped, there are Cast Members at each station to help out.

Collect your own "merit badges" (which are really stickers for your book) at stations all around the park. There are 30 of them in total, and this entire experience doesn't cost a penny!

This activity is fun for the entire family. You don't have to collect all 30 badges in one day, either; you can continue where you left off when you return on your next Disney Vacation!

Disney KiteTails

Have you ever tried to fly a kite? Well, you've never seen kites like these! Disney uses giant three-dimensional kites and windcatchers designed to look like you're favorite characters in this exciting show.

Watch Simba, Baloo and others dance through the air to your favorite Disney tunes. You can even sing along!

DinoLand U.S.A.

While DinoLand U.S.A. officially closed as a land, there are still some attractions in the area.

The Boneyard

Let your imagination soar, as you release your inner archaeologist.

The Boneyard is a giant, dino-themed playground at the entrance of Dinoland. Dig around the sand at a dinosaur excavation site, find mammoth bones and learn how they became extinct!

Better yet, jump on the giant dino footprints to hear a roar! You can even try out the Xylophone made from dino bones. It plays music when you press them.

If you want to burn off some more energy, climb the rope maze and race down the slippery slides.

Explorers will want to check out the rickety gate bridge that looks just like a real dinosaur skeleton.

Young kids can get lost for hours in the fun, but older kids want to rush further into DinoLand to experence the *DINOSAUR* ride!

DINOSAUR

The main attraction inside DinoLand is *DINOSAUR*. It's thrilling and maybe even a little scary with so many of the exciting Audio-Animatronic giants roaming around the dark!

On this ride, you travel back in time to the last few seconds of the Earth's *Cretaceous Period* (which was when dinosaurs still roamed the planet). Your mission is to bring back a live iguanadon (a type of dinosaur).

Be careful, though. A scary carnotaurus is on the hunt to make you his final meal, while the giant meteoroid that caused dinosaurs to go extinct (die out) is about to hit Planet Earth! Will you make it back in time?

Your time rover (ride vehicle) goes really fast over rough terrain. Hold on! When a Meteor shower hits, things get a bit bumpy!

Car•no•taur - ˈkärnəˌtôr/
Noun, plural: carnotaurs

Carnotaurus is a specific genus (identity of animal type). It's the animal with the stubby face and the little horns. Derived from the Latin word, carno ("which means meat or flesh") and taurus ("bull"), the name Carnotaurus means "meat-eating bull"

Don't confuse it with the group of theropods called Carnosaurs. These include Allosaurus and Carcharodontosaurus, though not Carnotaurus.

Car•no•saur - ˈkärnəˌsôr/
noun
plural: carnosaurs

Carnosaur is a large bipedal (walking on two legs), carnivorous (meat-eating) dinosaur, typically one with greatly shortened forelimbs.

The giant, spiny carnotaurus looks especially ferocious with its flaring nostrils. It pops out when you least expect it and is as ugly as it is scary! This dino has the stubby horns of a bull, the face of a toad and (short, squirrel-like) forelimbs (arms). We are told it's the largest Audio-Animatronic animal Disney Imagineers ever built!

DINOSAUR may not be for everyone. Many kids get freaked out in the dark, and it gets more and more scary. Remember, it's all make-believe! The ride gets rough and jerky, but it just makes it more exciting for everyone.

Really small, timid kids may not enjoy this at all.

Minimum Height Required:
40" tall (3 feet, 4 inches)

Finding Nemo: The Big Blue...And Beyond!

Just outside of Dino-Rama is an amazing show! This colorful, musical production is located in a theater called Theater in the Wild.

Clap your hands along with the musical beat, while you watch all of your favorites from the *Finding Nemo* movie, including Nemo's father, Dory and, of course, the little clownfish himself!

The 40-minute show is set to fun music in an "underwater" setting. The special effects make it seem real!

Kids especially love the giant, colorful puppets, flying acrobats and fun dancers! Parents enjoy that it's like a Broadway show - and in true Disney fashion, there are always fun tunes that you should know the words to - so sing-along!

This musical play is performed several times per day – see the Times Guide for specific times on the day of your visit. It is popular, so arrive early.

This show may be too long for really young kids, unless they are big fans of the little fish.

The theater is dark and cool - which makes it a great spot for a break on hot summer days (or a great napping spot if you've got a baby brother or sister).

Asia

At Disney's Animal Kingdom, Asia is represented with jungles, rainforests and animals, of course!

Feeling hot? Just listen for the sound of raging river rapids to cool off… that's right, you have the opportunity to get wet! Just hop into a raft on the Kali River Rapids.

The Animal Kingdom's biggest thrill (and fright!) can also be found here. Expedition Everest is the most intense roller coaster ride at the park (and possibly all of Disney World). It is scary-fun!

Did you know? Asia is the continent that makes up most of the landmass on our planet. In other words, it's huge. You might be surprised to learn it's twice the size of the United States!

Most people think of China and Japan when they think of Asia, It has way many more countries than that, including India and even a part of Russia.

If shows are more your thing, check out *Feathered Friends in Flight*. This is a very entertaining, yet educational, performance. It features real, live birds!

Maharajah Jungle Trek

Asia has some of the most majestic animals on Earth. It's fitting, therefore, that the setting for this walk-through zoo exhibit is a former palace. Take a short walk through the verdant (thick green) jungles of Asia in the *Maharajah Jungle Trek*.

Did you know that some dragons are real? You won't believe it until you check out the real Komodo dragon. Its venom is very dangerous against humans. Don't worry, though. This dragon can't get anywhere near you!

Look closely to spot the deer - they're pretty quiet and blend well into their surroundings.

About half-way through your trek is Disney's version of a bat cave, home to giant fruit bats. (Their favorite meal is melons!) Bats usually just sleep during the day, so look for them hanging upside down from a tree branch, using their sharp claws. There are hundreds of them!

If you are fortunate enough to see one of these bats fly, take note of the really long wingspan! Only a metal wire barrier separates the bats' home from visitors, though you might think they should have added glass to keep the stinky odor in! Even if you don't like bats (or their smell), there are places to view them from far, far away!

The most popular exhibit is the big family of tigers living in "ancient" temple ruins. Cast Members stand nearby with fun facts about the tigers, and they are eager to answer your questions.

Hidden Mickey Alert!

Look for Mickey hiding on a mural near the tigers.

Plan one more stop on the trail before you leave: an oasis with more birds than you can imagine! Pick up a bird guide before entering the aviary (bird enclosure). This will help you identify and name each and every colorful bird you find on your journey. A Cast Member is nearby to help, too!

Every little detail is planned out. You may notice lush plants, bamboo, bushes and trees - all were purposefully planted to give the real feel of Asia!

Expedition Everest

Looking off to the horizon, you can see the Forbidden Mountain. This Himalayan peak is the tallest mountain at Walt Disney World and home to the famous Abominable Snowman (called *Yeti* in Asia).

Do you have the nerve to ride this wild coaster and possibly encounter the beast? Your leisurely train ride through the snow-capped Forbidden Mountain soon becomes intense and fast-paced.

Did you know? It's fitting that Expedition Everest's mountain is the tallest in Disney World. It's namesake, Mount Everest is the tallest on the planet!

This fast coaster is rated among the top five by kids everywhere! It's quite a thrilling trip. There's even a section that goes backward… as you travel through the dark, deep recesses of the mountain!

While racing through the mountain peaks, you just might catch a glimpse of the Yeti. Hold on tight (better yet, put your arms up!) as you encounter the large, fast drop down the side of the mountain. Smile big - a camera catches your look of fear and delight!

Zipping along at top speeds, you might not catch all of the cool visual details. Try to keep your eyes open long enough to check out the caverns inside the mountain, the forested canyons around the outside and even the waterfalls.

Keep looking up while you race through the mountain, or you just may miss a face-to-face encounter with the giant and angry, ape-like creature.

Expedition Everest has more speed than Thunder Mountain, yet the track is pretty smooth. Just keep in mind there are a couple of intense jerks. This ride is wild, crazy, dark and scary!

Are you brave enough to face your fears?!

Family members that don't meet the height requirements (or bravery requirements) can watch the crazy train riders zip down the mountain from just outside the ride (although it's way funner to experience it for yourself).

Minimum Height Required:
44" tall (3 feet, 8 inches)

Kali River Rapids

Need to cool off in the intense Florida heat? You're bound to get soaked on Kali River Rapids!

This water raft ride starts out as a peaceful trip through the rain forest, but then gets fast and fun. Hold on tight as your raft drops over the small waterfalls!

Try to pay attention to your surroundings, while your raft bumps along the rocky sides and bobs up and down in the water. There's actually an important environmental message about deforestation you can easily miss while having fun.

While waiting in the queue (and briefly during the ride) you see how logging in the rain forests is having a devastating effect on the environment. (Logging is cutting down the trees for lumber, to make houses and buildings.) You even see some timber (logs) burning and catch a waft (or smell) of real smoke!

Lots of people leave this ride completely soaked! You may think the drenching is over when you see the docking station up ahead, but there's still more fun to be had! Take note of the stone elephants near the end of the journey. People standing on the bridge use buttons to shoot water at you from the elephants' trunks. You can get in on the soaking action after you exit the ride!

It doesn't really matter where you sit in the raft. Every seat gets wet, while some get super drenched!

Even if a seat looks dry as you board, it just means the last person soaked all the water up on their clothes.

Have a towel and a spare set of clothes handy, including shoes and socks. Or wear a poncho with clothes that dry easily. Leave anything you need to keep dry (including electronics and your change of clothes) in a locker near the entrance. It is free to use for up to 2 hours, so there's no reason not to take advantage of it.

You probably won't need to change your clothes if you're visiting on a super hot day, though. The hot sun will dry you off pretty quickly.

Minimum Height Required:
38" tall (3 feet, 2 inches)

Feathered Friends in Flight

Watch real birds do amazing *feats* on-stage. They soar high over the audience. If you're lucky, one may swoop down and almost touch your head!

Don't worry, though. The birds are very well trained to make sure they stay just out of reach.

This is a really unique and fun way to learn all about birds. They teach you everything you need to know about the flying critters.

The 25-minute show takes place several times daily at the Caravan Stage - check your Times Guide so you don't miss it.

Sometimes lucky kids who stay after the end of the show get to see a bird-in-training earn its wings and get a chance for fame.

Stick around for a few minutes, while the crowd clears out to see if a handler is going to do a special introduction.

This adventure takes place in a covered, outdoor theater - so you're in the shade, but keep in mind there's no air conditioning. It could get hot!

Africa

Get transported to the land of Simba, The Lion King. Disney's Imagineers spent months visiting the continent of Africa to make this section of the park incredible!

They visited forests and grasslands, and observed hundreds of different animals throughout their investigation. This is one of the most detailed and authentic areas in all of Disney World!

The best ways to see a lot of animals include riding Kilimanjaro Safaris, visiting Rafiki's Planet Watch by train and strolling along the Gorilla Falls walking trail - all found in Africa!

Kilimanjaro Safaris

Hop aboard an authentic safari truck and take a wild adventure through the jungles and plains of Africa! Explore the many different ecosystems that animals make home. Even better — observe animals that people hardly ever get to see in person.

On your safari, be sure to spot the lions, elephants and rhinos (rhinoceros). Zebras can also be spotted on the safari.

These animals aren't locked in a cage. They are free roaming and sometimes come right up to your safari vehicle! Remember, animals crossing the road as you pass by always have the right of way!

Of course, Disney makes sure every single animal is comfortable and safe, whether it's day or night. Most of the animals sleep indoors at night (in giant behind-the-scenes barns).

While animals are brought out during the day, they are never forced into the open. Instead, they are provided specific things to encourage them to stay visible to people, such as hidden feeding stations in logs and rocks. The lion pride actually has a cool air conditioner that makes them comfy atop their tall hillside home. This, in turn, makes them more likely to stay visible for everyone to see!

Look out for the humongous hippos (hippopotamus) swimming in pools. Did you know that these giants spend a lot of their lives staying cool under water? They breathe regular air, so you see them surface every few minutes to get a breath, but they rarely get all the way out of the water.

Nearby, find the frolicking flock of flamingos. Did you know they're pink because of the pigments in the food they eat? Flamingos would be white or grey without eating tiny brine shrimp, which turns the flamingos their bright color! They also eat crustaceans, algae and aquatic plants.

Out on the savannah, watch mama and baby giraffes eating leaves high in the trees.

Matching the animals' habitat and grazing habits is something that Disney folks know how to do! Trees and plants are available as natural meals, but there are also plants that get replaced all the time to make certain the animals always have enough fresh greens to eat.

This is a unique experience that is not to be missed! It's very safe to travel in your safari truck, which is really tall and has excellent traction. The trip isn't too fast. In fact, you barely drive over five miles per hour.

Be prepared to shoot dozens of pictures!

Gorilla Falls Exploration Trail

Next to the safari is a wandering or meandering, walking trail through the jungle. Take your time as you meander along the paths and spot several different types of animals!

While exploring at your own pace, look for the backside of the hippo's watering hole. You can see those and many of the same grazing animals from the Safari as you wander through.

If you love fish, check out the giant tanks. They are teeming with them. There's even a bird aviary (the name for a bird's home environment) you get to explore! Be sure to grab the printed bird guide when you enter the aviary. This will help you identify each colorful creature.

Keep an eye out for Timon's cousins at the meerkat exhibit. (These are small rodent-like animals, in case you've never seen The Lion King.)

> **Did you know?** Meerkats and warthogs don't actually get along well together. Pumbaa must be extra nice for Timon to be his friend!

What would the Gorilla Falls Exploration Trail be without gorillas?

There are a couple of different areas where gorillas call home. That's because Disney needs to keep the male silverbacks (named for the silver fur on their backs) apart from the gorilla families, since they can get aggressive.

Sometimes, these big and strong apes are just as interested in us as we are in them. Other times they just ignore us as they play with one another. If you are lucky, you might spy a baby gorilla with its mother.

Did you know? Gorilla *genes* are not that different from human ones. That is why they look kind of similar, with the shape of their faces, ears and bodies. In fact, both humans and gorillas are classified as apes!

Kid's Trivia!

Until 2016, this was called the Pangani Forest Expedition Trail [Pronounced Pawn-gone'-ee, with emphasis on the second syllable].

A Celebration of Festival of the Lion King

Tucked away in the farthest corner of Africa is a giant theater. Don't miss the show here: *Festival of the Lion King*. This is a wild and colorful musical and acrobatic spectacle starring all of your favorites from *The Lion King* film. See all the major characters, including Simba, Pumbaa and Timon.

During the show, look for The Lion King himself, Simba, sitting atop Pride Rock. His buddy, Pumbaa the wisecracking warthog looks over the crowd from a different corner. These two characters emcee the show, which takes place on stages made of large platforms that are basically parade floats. (In fact, they were once used in a parade at Disneyland!) Because they are on wheels, they can easily be moved onto the stage when they are needed.

Unlike many stage shows in Disney World that copy the movies they're named after, this is a unique extravaganza. It is a Broadway-type show with colorful costumes and puppets - your entire family will be amazed!

Gymnasts are dressed up like monkeys, and birds entertain the crowd with aerial (in the air) acrobatics. Professional singers will have you tapping your toes and clapping along to your favorite Lion King hits! This performance is very fun for kids… and grown-ups too!

Rafiki's Planet Watch

Travel on the Wildlife Express Train for a short backstage journey to Rafiki's Planet Watch. Once there, discover how you can help our planet and its animals survive, view animals being cared for at a real veterinary clinic and spend some time at the petting zoo!

Board your train at the station in Africa. This short trip is the only time most guests ever get to see behind-the-scenes at Disney.

View the large, high-tech barns that the safari animals call home when they are not performing on stage. This is where most animals receive care and sleep each night.

The Animation Experience at Conservation Station

Budding artists and conservationists love this attraction. Not only can you learn about the real-life animal inspirations for many Disney characters, but you also learn how to draw one!

This experience features a real Disney artist who walks you through the step-by-step process of drawing the featured character. They make it so simple, even an amateur can come away with a great work of art!

Come back again and again to test your skills with new characters. It's such great fun!

Hallway of Animal Health and Care

There is an actual, working animal hospital (meaning it's where Disney's many animals get medical care when it is needed). You might even see veterinarians (animal doctors) examine or treat their patients. Keep an eye out for the small animals who call this clinic home.

Throughout the building are exhibits. Some are educational, such as those that teach about conservation. Other exhibits are interactive. Pay attention. You just might learn how to find out about conservation efforts near where you live!

Check your Times Guide as Rafiki likes to make an appearance for pictures and autographs! And just outside, you might run into Chip & Dale, too!

Affection Section

Grab a brush and find a goat or sheep to groom. In this fun, outdoor area everyone can pet and groom real barnyard animals, such as goats and sheep.

Remember to wash your hands! Because the creatures in the Affection Section can be dirty, there's a large washing station as you exit. Use it, or you may be mistaken for a stinky goat!

Pandora

Get ready to leave this world and enter another land, one unlike any you have ever seen before.

Travel to Pandora: World of Avatar. In this alien landscape, you get to walk under floating mountains and around waterfalls, see plants that glow at night (called bioluminescent), hear unique animal sounds,

play native drums and ride some of Disney's coolest rides!

Pandora: World of Avatar is the Animal Kingdom's newest land, which opened on May 27, 2017. It is based on the movie, Avatar, that was released in 2009. The official name of this land is the Valley of Mo'ara. It is where the Na'vi people live in peace with humans and celebrate all that nature has to offer.

You enter Pandora either on a bridge by Tiffins Restaurant or from behind The Lion King show. Either way, be ready to see and hear things from a far-off planet.

The land and sounds become less earth-like and more alien the closer you get to the middle of the Valley of Mo'ara. Sometimes it can be really hard to tell which plants are real planet Earth plants and which ones were created by Imagineers for the land.

This is definitely a great place to explore. Pay attention to everything — you never know what you might discover!

Kid's Tip!

If you don't have a Lightning Lane reservation for Flight of Passage, use the My Disney Experience app to watch the queue wait times throughout the day. You may find the shortest times first thing in the morning and during the nighttime show. However, you can also jump into line just a few minutes before the park closes. As long as you're in line before closing time, you can wait as long as it takes to get on the ride. The best part is you won't have wasted hours waiting in line when you could have been enjoying other attractions!

Pandora is really large, so plan some time to just explore it. There are plants you can interact with and all kinds of old artifacts to see. There is also a fun place to eat with unique and interesting foods, like cheeseburger pods and blue cheesecake. If you're daring, you should try them. (Don't worry, they have some normal foods, too.)

Kid's Tip!

If you have to wait in a long line, make sure to use the bathroom facilities first. Unlike most rides, *Flight of Passage* has a bathroom in the line queue if you can't wait.

In the middle of all of this land is a huge drum area. Join in while the local musicians of Pandora put on a lively show each day. Feel free to play the drums and bang out your own tunes even when there isn't a show.

Kid's Tip!

If you are taking part in the Wilderness Explorers Challenge at Animal Kingdom, be on the lookout for a Wilderness Explorers station in Pandora. There are fun activities that allow you to earn Pandora badges as you learn [illegible]nts that live in the Valley

Kid's Tip!

If you can, visit Pandora both during the daytime and nighttime. At night, the land completely changes the way it looks, because all of the plants light up with bioluminescence. Even the pathway glows!

Avatar: Flight of Passage

You won't want to miss this high-tech attraction. It is very thrilling to ride on the back of a Banshee and fly through the Valley of Mo'ara. While it is no more extreme than Soarin' at Epcot, the simulation and realistic ride motion makes it one of the most exciting rides in all of Disney World.

Did you know? Banshees aren't the only *mythological* (based on legend) creatures in the Animal Kingdom. Take a close look at the benches around the park to find dragons. Disney planned to have a whole section of the park devoted to dragons, but changed their minds. They left the winged creatures on the benches as a reminder of the original idea!

Flight of Passage is located in the midle of Valley of Mo'Ara. It has one of the longest wait times in Disney World. Make this your number one *priority* for a Lightning Lane reservation. If you can't get one, be prepared to wait in line for hours.

As you wait for the ride, you get to weave through incredible waterfalls and plants and then into an underground cave. Look all around you for proof of the Na'vi that have visited here before, like the paintings on the walls.

You know you're getting close when you enter the laboratory. This is where scientists study Pandora and all its wonders. There are tons of signs to read and things to see, like a life-size avatar floating in a tube of liquid!

When you're near the actual ride, your group will be brought into a training room and told all about how they link you to your personal Avatar. Finally, you get to the ride!

You get your own personal vehicle that kind of looks like a mini motorcycle without wheels. You sit on it just like a bike. Once you're in place, put on your 3D goggles and hold onto the handlebars. The restraints will secure you into your seat, so there's no way to fall off!

The large screen will open up in front of you, the floor will disappear and off you fly through Pandora on a Mountain Banshee! It is beautiful and fun and kind of scary, but remember, it's just a 3-D movie. You're perfectly safe for the whole thing!

Fun Fact! You can actually feel the Banshee breathing between your legs and smell the scents of the Valley of Mo'ara.

This is a very *unique* ride. There are some important things you need to know:

1) Once you get through the queue, you will be riding alone. Only one person is allowed on a seat at a time, so it's impossible to hold Mom or Dad's hand if you get scared.
2) This is a 3-D, fully immersive ride. That means once you're on the actual Banshee, you will feel like you are truly flying. If you get car sick or

easily queasy, this ride might not be the best for you. (Close your eyes. That will help!)

3) There are several unique restraints to keep you safe. If you don't like being restrained (your legs get locked into place), then you might not like this ride.

Now, if you've read all of that, and you're thinking "I'm ready," then prepare to have the most incredible ride of your life!

Minimum Height Required:
44" tall (3 feet, 8 inches)

Na'vi River Journey

This short, peaceful boat ride is found deep inside the Valley of Mo'ara, which can make the entrance a bit hard to find. That's okay, though. It's such a fun land, you won't mind getting a little lost in it!

> **Did you know?** When Disney first opened Pandora: World of Avatar, they didn't have any directional signs, just Na'vi totems to show the way. While the totems are very cool, many people got lost, so now there are signs you can follow!

This ride has no height requirement, so everyone in the family can go on it!

The line queue for *Na'vi River Journey* is very cool with lots of things to look at and learn. You can read about all of the animals and plants found on your journey.

Once on your boat, there's so much to see! Unique Pandora creatures appear on the paths surrounding the water, some looking fierce and others friendly.

Look all around and even up above to see the many incredible sights and beautiful colors. The ride ends as you pass by the Shaman, one of the highest tech Audio-Animatronics in the world! She is called the Na'vi Shaman of Songs and will send you off with positive energy.

Fun Facts: Learn some Na'vi language while you're there:

English Word	Na'Vi Word
Hello	Kaltxi [Kahl-T'IH]
My name is	Oeru Syaw [WEH-roo syow]
Thanks	Irayo [EE-ra-yo]
Please	Rutxe [roo-T'EH]

Entertainment

DiVine (Only During Busy Times)

DiVine is a tall, "tree person" that comes to life. She wanders through the crowd very slowly, just how you might imagine a tree would move if it could pick up its roots and walk around.

She walks on stilts, so she hovers way above everyone. Her leaves provide camouflage, and she moves so slowly and silently that many people don't notice until she's right next to them!

If you spot her, take a step back and watch her - sometimes she's funny and plays tricks on unsuspecting people. It's amazing how many people rush by her without ever knowing she's right there!

Tam Tam Drummers of Harambe

In Harambe, African drummers share their cultural beats and sing tribal songs. They just might invite you to dance along or even beat a drum!

Kid's Tip!

Because a lot of the park is outdoors, along walking trails and such, you can get extra hot and thirsty, especially in the middle of summer. Remember to take a micro-break for a couple of sips of water every few minutes!

Bollywood Beats

Song and dance is a huge part of Indian culture, and this lively troupe (a group of entertainers) wants you to experience the best of it! What would music be without dance? Dancers pull guests from the crowd to teach a lively dance step or two in Asia!

Viva Gaya Street Band

Also in Asia, an exciting musical troupe sings and dances with uniquely Asian music. You won't be able to stop your feet from moving to the beat!

Pandora Rangers

Is that a robot walking around Pandora? It's a conservation scientist in a crazy utility suit! Watch him tower over the crowd, as he wades through amazed onlookers. The Transformers have nothing on this guy!

Winged Encounters - The Kingdom Takes Flight

Who doesn't love parrots? Disney experts have trained these amazing birds to put on a show above the Tree of Life several times a day. Watch them circle the sky before coming to rest on their perches below.

Tree of Life Awakenings

When the sun goes down, the Tree of Life comes to life. Watch several times each night as the leaves change colors and different animal stories are displayed in brilliant color. You may find your mouth hanging open in awe! Check your Times guide for showtimes.

Character Meet & Greets

Adventurer's Outpost (Discovery Island) is one of *THE COOLEST* places to meet **Mickey** and **Minnie** at Walt Disney World! They invite guests into their air-conditioned summer home all day long!

Rafiki's Planet Watch often has unique characters, but they change regularly. You may see **Jiminy Cricket** or find **Doc McStuffins** on-hand to help treat what ails your toys!

Chester & Hester's Dino-Rama (DinoLand, U.S.A.) is where **Goofy** and **Pluto** greet people. **Donald Duck** can be found not too far away.

Russell and **Dug** are excited to meet you near the entrance to *It's Tough to be a Bug*. Keep searching the area to find **Timon** and **Pumbaa**!

Princess lovers will find only one at Animal Kindom. Find the enchanting **Pocahontas** at *Character Landing* in Discovery Island.

ATTRACTION RATINGS

Super Cool (MUST-SEE)	Cool (SHOULD SEE)	Fun (SEE IF YOU CAN)
Avatar Flight of Passage	Na'vi River Journey	-none-
Expedition Everest	Flights of Wonder	
Kilimanjaro Safaris	The Boneyard Playground	
Dinosaur	The Affection Section (at Rafiki's Planet Watch)	
Maharajah Jungle Trek	Finding Nemo, The Musical	
Kali River Rapids	The Oasis	
Festival of the Lion King	TriceraTop Spin	
It's Tough to be a Bug!	Disney KiteTails	
Gorilla Falls Exploration Trail		

If you notice, there are no "See if You Can" things listed. This is because you should have plenty of time to see everything you want to in one full day at the Animal Kingdom (if you use your Lightning Lane reservations!).

Animal Kingdom Favorites

Across

2. This type of big cat is found in Asia.

3. This type of big cat is found in Africa.

5. A paleontologist digs up bones of what type of animal?

6. Known for its conservation efforts, Animal Kingdom opened on _________ Day in 1998.

7. Take a ride on this alien creature in Pandora.

9. The Tree of __________ is the Animal Kingdom's park icon.

10. Come face to face with the _________ (Abominable Snowman) while climbing the Forbidden Mountain.

Down

1. The glowing plants in Pandora are known as _________.

4. What mythical creature is found on some benches at Animal Kingdom?

8. Take a real African _________ to see wild animals in Disney's Animal Kingdom

*Answers on Page 210

Other Fun Stuff at Disney World (and Other Nearby Places)

You've already read through the sections on the theme parks, so you know all about the great shows and parades.

We've also mentioned a lot of the other fun things to do. Here are a few more things you can enjoy at Disney World.

Water Parks

Do you think there are only four theme parks in Disney World? Not so!

There are actually six, as there are two super-fun water parks. Both have whimsical themes - Typhoon Lagoon and Blizzard Beach! These wet adventure parks are lushly landscaped; they contain pools, adrenaline-charged water slides, raft rides, interactive fountains and lazy rivers that take you on a relaxing trip around the parks!

Take water shoes with you, so you don't burn your toes or ruin your good sneakers.

Blizzard Beach and Typhoon Lagoon are two of the biggest and best water parks in the world. They are both open most of the year (because the weather is almost always hot in Florida!), and even when one is closed for refurbishment, the other is still open.

Chilling in a lazy river or wave pool can be a laid back way to enjoy the refreshing water. Try a water coaster for more intense fun!

Can't decide which park you want to visit? If you get a ticket to one water park, you can visit both on the same day! (This is a feature called *Park Hopping.*)

On super-hot summer days, it is easy to spend an entire day in your bathing suit.

Kid's Tip!

Remember to drink lots of water and don't forget to apply sunscreen often. It's especially easy to forget when you're playing in the water, and you're more likely to get a nasty sunburn at a pool. Ouch!

Typhoon Lagoon

This water park looks like it was hit by a huge typhoon, which is the point.

The storm was so severe that a shrimp boat named Miss Tilly ended up teetering all the way to the top of a mountain!

"A furious storm once roared cross the sea

Catching ships in its path, helpless to flee

Instead of a certain and watery doom

The wind swept them here to Typhoon Lagoon."

Did you know? A typhoon is commonly known as a hurricane. People just use different names for them based on the ocean where the storm occurs: typhoons occur in the Northwest Pacific Ocean, while hurricanes take place in the Atlantic and Northeast Pacific oceans.

The word hurricane actually comes from the name of the Caribbean god of evil: Hurrican. In a typhoon, you get super strong winds and lots of rain. Florida residents know all about this. The state gets hit by hurricanes often!

Typhoon Lagoon has an enormous wave pool – the biggest in North America! Its waves reach six feet high, way over most people's heads!

It's so much fun to body-surf here! If you want a bigger challenge, early morning surf lessons are available to teach you how to "hang ten" on a surfboard. These lessons take place on select mornings before the park opens to the public. Ask your parents to make a reservation!

At Typhoon Lagoon, there's a lot that you can do with your family! Compete as you race down a speed slide, or slip down Crush 'n' Gusher, a thrilling roller coaster slide. You can even hop aboard an inner tube (an inflatable donut) and take a trip around the lazy river that goes all around the park.

Smaller kids have a special place called Ketchakiddee Creek with kid-sized slides and other fun.

Blizzard Beach

Did you know that there is a snow-covered mountain in Florida?

Luckily it's not real snow in this ski resort, and you won't freeze when you wear your bathing suit.

Rather than ski down the mountain, you get to travel down a huge water slide. You can even take a real chair-lift up to the top of Mount Gushmore - at the top is a great view of the entire park, not to mention some of the best water slides in the world!

Summit Plummet

Summit Plummet is probably the scariest slide at the water parks! In fact, it's the third tallest body water slide in the whole world!

The top platform looks like a ski-jump - but that's just for decoration. Each rider experiences a drop going straight down practically at *Highway Speeds*! Try not to look down, as you start your descent from 120 feet in the sky before reaching speeds of 60 miles per hour. That is about as fast as cars travel down the highway!

This water slide contains a 60 degree angle (that's close to vertical!) and a 12-story drop!

If *Summit Plummet* looks too intimidating, there are other methods for getting back down the mountain - thank goodness!

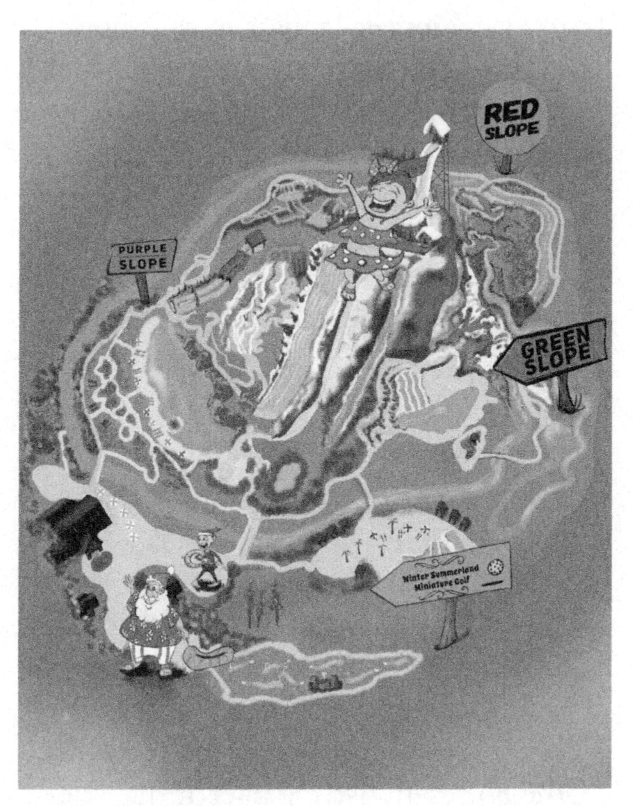

Slush Gusher

Right next to *Summit Plummet* is *Slush Gusher*, another really tall body slide. This one only reaches 35 miles per hour and has a couple of dips and humps, causing you to actually get a little air time!

Teamboat Springs

Another super fun way to get down the mountain is riding *Teamboat Springs* with your whole family! This is the world's longest family white-water raft ride (up to 6 people in a raft). This allows everyone to twist and turn down the mountain in a fun and exciting way!

Other Attractions

On the back of Mount Gushmore are tube slides. On the side of the mountain are the Toboggan Racers and Storm Racers - these are mat-slides. If you have the energy, you can spend all day going up and down this mountain!

Want to stay at the base of the mountain for a bit? Preteens Ski Patrol Training Camp has an "iceberg" obstacle course and rope swings to drop into the water.

Tike's Peak is a special part of the park just for youngsters with smaller slides and a snow-castle, fountain play area.

Blizzard Beach Legend tells of a freak snow storm that hit Orlando many years ago. One enterprising man was quick to create a ski resort to *capitalize* on (meaning to take advantage of) the icy conditions. No sooner did the resort get built than the hot Florida sun came back, ruining his plans! The snow melted, turning the slopes to rushing water. Not to be discouraged, the man realized he now had a splendid water park on his hands!

Fort Wilderness

Maybe you're not into water slides? That's perfectly okay. There are tons of other fun things around Disney!

Fort Wilderness is Disney's campground area. It's located in a wooded area close to Wilderness Lodge, a huge resort.

Families can stay at the campgrounds overnight or just show up for a day. Some people stay for months-on-end!

If you love animals and nature, you should visit the ranch. There are wild deer roaming the property and a real ranch with horses. It's free to stop by.

Fort Wilderness is a tranquil, relaxing place to get away from the noise and "hustle and bustle" of the theme parks.

Tri-Circle-D Ranch

https://disneyworld.disney.go.com/recreation/tri-circle-d-ranch/

Kids of all ages love riding painted ponies on the Magic Kingdom's Prince Charming Regal Carrousel. Most have no idea they can hop into the saddles of real ponies and horses at the Tri-Circle-D Ranch at Fort Wilderness.

Have you ever wondered where the horses that pull the trolley around the Magic Kingdom live? They live in a large barn near Pioneer Hall. You can show up to say hello to them. Kids older than nine years old can also ride a trail on horseback (for a fee)!

These horses also pull horse-drawn wagons and the carriages at some of the resorts.

Adults often take romantic carriage rides on special occasions. (Around Halloween and Christmas, there is a particularly special ride on a horse-drawn wagon that is made especially for families!)

The horses you see on Disney property are cared for by the same people that drive the wagons and carriages. That's because they form a very special bond of friendship and trust, so they work well together.

The horses all live together at the Tri-Circle-D Ranch, which is located along the canals that feed into Bay Lake and the Seven Seas Lagoon. This is close to where you can rent a motorboat or canoe to play on the water. It's also a great place for young kids to fish. (We talk more about this in a bit.)

Chip 'n' Dale's Campfire Sing-A-Long

This (completely free!) show is one of Disney's best kept secrets!

Each night your family can gather around a campfire, sing songs and meet Chip and Dale! There is a small fee for supplies if you'd like to join in a marshmallow roast and make ooey gooey s'mores. Yum!

Dinner Show

If you really want some foot-stompin' fun, Fort Wilderness is has a dinner show that kids love called *Hoop-Dee-Doo Musical Revue.*

Get ready to clap your hands and sing along with Mickey and a bunch of his friends.

The show with dinner is pretty expensive, so it's great for a special event, like a birthday.

Plan to see it on a day when you have nothing else planned (called an "off day" or "down day"). That will give you plenty of time to explore all the other neat things to do at Fort Wilderness. Yee haw!

Bay Lake Water Fun

https://disneyworld.disney.go.com/recreation/motorized-boats

Your family can rent boats and zip around the lake. Take a mini speed boats (called a "Sea Raycer") for a spin, or get a larger pontoon boat for a relaxing day on the water!

Minimum Height and Age Required

You must be 18 years or older to rent a boat by yourself. If you can convince a parent to rent one of the Sea Raycers, and you are at least 12 years old and 60 inches (5 feet tall), you can steer the boat yourself - how awesome!

Kids love these fast boats, but the ride can get a little bumpy. Hold on tight and watch out for other boats! This costs about $45 per half hour.

Fishing

https://disneyworld.disney.go.com/recreation/fishing/

Walt Disney World offers guided fishing excursions as well as dockside fishing. It's catch-and-release only. Give it a try. Just don't let Nemo or Dory know!

Miniature Golf - Disney Style!

https://disneyworld.disney.go.com/recreation/winter-summerland-miniature-golf/

Adults may want to play real golf at one of Disney's championship golf courses. Two ultra-decked out mini-golf attractions are way more fun for kids! Winter Summerland has a Christmas-theme, while Fantasia Gardens patterns itself on the classic Disney animated film. Each has two separate 18-hole courses for a great challenge.

Both mini-golf locations are fun to play for people of all ages!

Disney's Winter Summerland

When Santa Claus and his elves need to vacation, this is where they visit. Santa built these mini-golf courses as a place to relax when their busy schedule gives them time.

There are two Christmas-themed courses: Summer or Winter!

The Summer course is beach themed, complete with surf boards and castles.

It has the more challenging, trickier holes. First-timers might want to start with the easier Winter course. (You even get a glimpse of Santa resting at the hardest hole on the course! You have to get the ball to roll across his chest without waking him up. If you do, you might end up on his *Naughty List*.)

As a reminder of their home at the North Pole, the elves built a second course that looks like it is covered in snow. Putt your ball around (or through) Igloos, Happy snowmen and even holes for ice fishing!

Mickey makes a surprise appearance after you get your ball into one of the cups!

There is a small fee to play:
$12 for one round for kids 3-9
$14 for people 10 years and older

Fantasia Gardens

Only one of the mini-golf courses here is based on the classic Disney film named Fantasia. Around the course are dancing mushrooms, hippos dancing ballet on their tiptoes, stairs made of xylophones and even holes grouped by musical themes.

There's even a 'Dance of the Hours' hole. For example, you get to see a hippo standing on top of an alligator. Once you get your golf ball into the alligator's mouth, the hippo does a little dance!

If you think mini golf is too easy, the second course is specially designed to challenge even experienced golf pros. It's a real golf course made miniature. It even has real grass and sand!

There is a small fee to play:
$12 for one round for kids 3-9
$14 for people 10 years and older

Sports

If you love to play sports, there are lots of things to do around Disney World. You can stay active by riding bikes, exploring playgrounds, trekking through the forest trails at Fort Wilderness or jogging around the Boardwalk.

ESPN Wide World of Sports Complex

Sports nuts won't want to miss seeing this huge facility. It was designed as a place to play almost any sport you can imagine.

It's so nice, the Atlanta Braves make the baseball diamonds their spring training home. They hold games there every year in March. (And, yes, you can watch if you're in town!)

You can show up any other day to watch amateur sporting events that are taking place. Tickets cost about $12 for kids 3-9 and $17 for anyone 10 years or older.

If you want to see a Major League game, you need advanced tickets. Prices vary, so have a parent call for information (407-939-4263).

The Baseball stadium has lawn seating. Bring a blanket and picnic lunch to enjoy the game.

Scavenger Hunts and Events Designed Just for Kids

Every day at Disney World is special, but there are ways to make it even more amazing.

Disney has lots of tours and special events available, which you can view at:

https://disneyworld.disney.go.com/events-tours/

Our top picks for kids are listed in this section. Each makes for a truly unique vacation.

Family Magic Tour

Have you ever been on a scavenger hunt? This means you search for items or clues as part of a fun game. The Family Magic Tour is a super-fun themed scavenger hunt. The whole family will enjoy this romp around the Magic Kingdom. In this game, each family is given clues. Your mission is to seek the answers to locate a missing item.

The Family Magic Tour is a two-hour long event; wear sneakers and bring something to drink!

The cost is $37 for each member of your party 3 years or older.

Ask a parent to call 407-WDW-TOUR (939-8987) for reservations.

Pirate Adventure Cruise

Pirate treasure has been buried around the Seven Seas Lagoon, you just need the map and a ship to go find it!

Adventures abound while you sail from different locations along the Seven Seas Lagoon (the big lake in front of the park) finding hidden treasures. The ship captain helps you along the way with puzzling clues.

A light snack is provided for you as you search for the ultimate loot.

Pirate Adventures take place at:

- Grand Floridian
- Caribbean Beach resort
- Yacht and Beach Club

This is a two-hour treasure hunt for kids 4-12 years old. The cost is $37 per child. Ask a parent to call 407-939-3463 for reservations.

Sense of Africa at Disney's Animal Kingdom Lodge

Learn all about one of Disney's coolest hotels and all the animals that call it home! Your whole family will enjoy eating a special breakfast at Boma in the Animal Kingdom Lodge, then setting off on a safari to see the giraffes and other animals living at the resort.

This is a three-and-a-half-hour tour for all ages. The cost is $250 per person. Ask a parent to call 407-939-7529 for reservations.

Wild Africa Trek

Trek into the African Forest on this guided tour at Disney's Animal Kingdom park! This special three-hour adventure takes guests off the beaten path. These small-group walking tours venture deep into the woods, providing up-close encounters with hippos, crocodiles and other animals. Cross a rope bridge, ride over the open African savannah, sample some African foods and even receive a fun souvenir!

You have to be at least 8 years old to do this adventure, and you need an adult with you if you're under 18. Instead of a minimum height requirement, this adventure has a minimum weight requirement! You have to be at least 45 pounds to make sure your harness fits properly, so eat lots of churros and ice cream if you're close!

This is a three-hour tour. The cost ranges from $189 to $249 per person, depending on the day and season.

Disney Springs

https://www.disneysprings.com/

Do you love shopping? How about eating? Who doesn't love getting thier groove on with live music and dance? Disney Springs is *the* place to shop, eat, dance and play!

Just like everything at Disney World, Disney Springs has its own unique theme. It looks like a real Florida town, complete with different neighborhoods!

Much of Disney Springs was built within the last few years. New shops and restaurants are added all the time. There's always something new to discover!

If you love to dance, you can nearly always find live music or a rockin' DJ (disk jockey). The famous House of Blues restaurant has concerts nearly every night. Check out their website to see who is playing and get tickets (*houseofblues.com/orlando*).

Wear your swimsuit under your clothes when you visit. There's a cool water feature made just for kids to hop around in the water!

It's pretty much impossible to get bored at Disney Springs. There are more food and retail locations than you can shake a stick at.

Smoothies and slushies can be found at many locations, including the AMC dine-in movie theater, where you can order and eat a full meal, all while watching a movie in a comfy recliner.

Entertainment

If you want a little more action, compete to see who is the best bowler at **Splitsville,** a two-story bowling alley. They serve really good food while you bowl!

Cirque du Soleil (a French term, pronounced 'Sirk do so-LAY' and meaning *circus of the sun*) is a gigantic stadium that looks like a tent. The enchanting circus show inside is put on by a theater company based in Montreal, Canada.

While you might see Cirque du Soleil shows all over the world, the only Disney-themed one is at Disney Springs in Walt Disney World!

The show features Disney animation, along with great performances by gymnasts, acrobats, and other circus performers. Be amazed by the breathtaking, physics-defying circus acts performed by a razzle-dazzle, resident troupe in the permanent tent. The giant stage moves all around in ways that are hard to explain!

Shopping

If you've got some money burning a hole in your pocket or super generous parents, the Marketplace is a fun shopping area with the largest Disney souvenir store on earth - called **World of Disney**! If you're looking for something in particular, this mega-store likely has it.

Once Upon a Toy is exactly how it sounds - a toy store full of Disney-themed toys. There's even a *Mr. Potato Head* station where you can fill a box full of Potato Head accessories!

We saved the best for last - there's a **LEGO** store! That's right - LEGOS! You can even play here without having to buy anything!

Food

With all the shopping and playing around, you're bound to get hungry. There's practically a place to eat around every corner in Disney Springs. Try **T-Rex** for a prehistoric meal surrounded by Audio-Animatronic dinosaurs.

The **Rainforest Cafe** is the wildest restaurant, where you eat in a rainforest surrounded by Audio-Animatronic gorillas, elephants and even cheetahs! Located in the Marketplace, you can watch the giant volcano behind The Rainforest Cafe erupt (it happens every 30 minutes)!

If you're just after a quick snack, have a parent help you order a cupcake from the coolest ATM in the world - the **Sprinkles** cupcake ATM!

Maybe you just need to quench your thirst. The **Coca-Cola Store** has a rooftop bar with Coke-flavored beverages. Youc an pick one up on your way to meet the famous Coca-Cola Bear (located inside the store)!

Disney Cruise Line

https://disneycruise.disney.go.com/

Want to go beyond the parks? Take a trip aboard a gigantic cruise ship with Mickey and all his friends!

You can sail to the Caribbean islands from Port Canaveral, which is just a short drive from Disney World. You can even stop for a day at Disney's very own island, called *Castaway Cay*. There are plenty of places to play in the ocean, run and scream!

And the swimming pools! There are so many fun pools aboard each Disney Cruise ship — one even has a water coaster!

There are also adult-only pools… in case mom and dad want a break from you kids. Don't worry, though. Disney has the best kids-only stuff on their ships to give you a fun time away from your parents!

Fun Stuff Outside of Disney

Disney World is so large that you can have an entire vacation and never have to leave their property! But, just because you're going to Disney doesn't mean you can't find other fun things to do.

Remember, Orlando is the Theme Park Capital of the World! That means there are loads of cool activities around.

Here are some other fun things to do around Florida.

Orlando Area

Universal Studios Orlando

Universal Studios has two amazing theme parks: **Universal Studios** and **Islands of Adventure**. You can ride roller coasters, play with little yellow minions or find out what it's like to be a wizard at Universal Studios!

Each theme park has different themed lands and amazing rides. Much like Disney, there is also a cool water park called **Volcano Bay** there.

Best yet, if you get a park-to-park pass (meaning you can go to more than one park per day), you can ride the exclusive *Hogwarts Express* ride. That's right, find out what it's like to be a wizard like Harry Potter as you travel from Diagon Alley in London to Hogsmeade and back again!

Sea World Orlando

Sea World Orlando is dedicated to all things related to the ocean. While it has lots of rides, it is more than just a theme park.

This is where you can learn all about sea life. Meet whales, dolphins, sea lions, sharks and many more aquatic forms of life. Many of the animals perform in shows!

If that's not enough, visit the North Pole at the Penguin Encounter. You can also travel on a moving walkway through a clear acrylic tube inside a 600,000-gallon aquarium in the "Sharks!" pavilion.

Of course, theme parks need rides. There are some great ones at Sea World, including *Mako* (named after the Mako shark). It's the tallest and fastest roller coaster in all of Orlando!

Nearby **Discovery Cove** is an all-inclusive water park owned by Sea World. You can swim with dolphins and enjoy all the water park has to offer.

Outside Orlando

Less than one-hour from Disney, you can reach Legoland, the Kennedy Space Center, Cypress Gardens and Daytona Beach. Just another 30 minutes gets you to Busch Gardens-Tampa and Florida's Silver Springs in Ocala.

Kennedy Space Center

Find out what it's like to go into outer space!

The **Kennedy Space Center** has been the East Coast launch point for space shuttles for decades.

For an amazing day, try an experience that lets you train like an astronaut or spend a day on a simulated Mars surface.

They offer different tours for you to think about. Go on the two-hour Red Tour for a bus ride to the Flight Crew Training Building and the Apollo 11 Moon Landing Show, the space shuttle and Apollo launch sites, and the 525-foot-tall Vehicle Assembly Building.

The Blue Tour transports you through the Cape Canaveral Air Force Station, including the Mercury and Gemini pads and the Air Force Space Museum.

Legoland

Legoland was built just for kids! It's great for anyone 12 and under, but especially great for those who love playing with Legos.

Go on rides and live out a Legoland adventure!

Did you know? Legoland was built on the former Cypress Gardens. They kept the botanical garden portion. You can still walk through it when you visit Legoland!

Daytona Beach

Great beaches and fast cars are what Daytona Beach is known for!

This is where the famous car race, the Daytona 500, is held every February. If you're visiting at a different time, you might see other races, including motorcycles and go-carts!

Sun and fun is what Florida does best. That's why most people to go Daytona for

Disney Fairies

T	E	M	L	I	G	L	I	S	S	R	Y	O	M
E	L	K	L	P	E	R	I	W	I	N	K	L	E
R	I	R	O	L	I	M	D	R	O	L	B	Y	L
E	E	D	L	N	O	N	P	R	I	L	L	A	C
N	Z	S	L	Z	K	S	B	E	C	E	A	A	S
C	A	O	E	A	D	E	E	D	H	A	F	T	I
E	L	R	B	R	R	E	C	P	E	A	A	T	L
R	B	S	R	I	F	A	K	P	E	S	I	E	V
B	F	O	E	N	I	A	N	A	S	S	R	S	E
E	S	F	K	A	R	S	R	I	E	E	Y	O	R
S	P	P	N	I	A	F	A	W	N	D	M	R	M
S	I	L	I	I	D	E	W	E	Y	I	A	D	I
I	K	A	T	A	E	R	A	R	R	R	R	N	S
T	E	T	E	C	E	A	A	L	M	I	Y	Y	T

FIRA
FAIRY MARY
PERIWINKLE
GLISS
LORD MILORI
FAWN
IRIDESSA
BESS
ZARINA
TINKER BELL
SPIKE
DEWEY
CHEESE
SILVERMIST
PRILLA
ROSETTA
TERENCE
BLAZE
BECK
RANI

the beach. It's a whopping 23-miles long and 500-feet wide, not to mention one of the most famous beaches in the world!

Busch Gardens - Tampa

If you're a real thrill-seeker, **Busch Gardens - Tampa** is home to some of the wildest rides anywhere! Try a roller coaster that drops straight down, or even a *drop ride* that faces you toward the ground before you plummet to your doom!

The other thing Busch Gardens is known for is animals. There are lots of them there. You can see a cheetah (at the base of its namesake roller coaster), kangaroos, apes, zebras and many others!

If you stay near Tampa, you may want to try Busch Gardens' water park, **Adventure Island**. It's got a wave pool, speed slide, flumes and more!

Florida's Silver Springs

Silver Springs is a state park that's known for its clear water and beauty. It's actually the world's largest formation of clear artesian springs, and it's located in central Florida!

You can take a tour of the river in a glass bottom boat. If you prefer to stay on land, try a Jeep safari through the wildlife preserve. You might spot monkeys, zebras and, of course, real Florida.

Fun Things to Do

Across

3. Ride a ________ across Seven Seas Lagoon.

5. Wave to Mickey and Minnie on top of their ________ float.

7. The best ice cream bars to eat are shaped like ________ Mouse!

8. Ride a fast ________ coaster.

10. Let's go ________ back riding at Fort Wilderness!

Down

1. If you want an autograph, get in line to meet a Disney ________.

2. The night sky lights up with Magic Kingdom's ________ show.

4. See real ________ in a safari.

6. Dress like a ________ and sing, "Yo Ho Ho."

9. Fantasia Gardens is a miniature ________ course.

*Answers on Page 213

Let's Eat at Disney World!

Kid Favorite Restaurants

Magic Kingdom:	Be Our Guest Restaurant; Cosmic Ray's Starlight Cafe
Epcot:	Akershus; Biergarten Restaurant; Space 220
Hollywood Studios:	Hollywood & Vine; Roundup Rodeo BBQ
Animal Kingdom:	Restaurantosaurus; Satu'li Canteen
Disney Springs:	T-Rex; Rainforest Cafe
Disney Hotels:	'Ohana; Chef Mickey's; 1900 Park Faire

Disney has plenty of healthy and delicious choices for kids. Look for this symbol at food service establishments to know what is especially yummy and healthy for you:

When people laugh at Mickey Mouse it's because he's so human; and that is the secret of his popularity.

- Walt Disney

Are you a budding foodie? Get ready to blog about your favorite Disney eats!

There are more places to find food than you can imagine. A lot of the food is stuff you've tried before, like burgers and pizzas.

If you look around, though, there are very different flavors than you may have encountered. Some of them have very strong spices and unique tastes.

If you don't like surprises, don't worry! Most restaurants have a special menu just for kids. Just ask the server! If you're not checking carbs, here are some favorite meal and snack options and locations where you can find them. The tasty treats on this list should satisfy the appetite of any kid:

Magic Kingdom

Restaurant (Location)	Food Type
Sweets	
Aloha Isle	Dole Whip Ice Cream
Aunti Gravity's Galactic Goodies	Smoothies
Gaston's Tavern (Fantasyland)	Cinnamon Rolls & LeFou's Brew (apple slushie drink)
Main Street Confectionary (Main Street, U.S.A.)	Cookies, Candy and Crispie Treats
Plaza Ice Cream Parlor (Main Street, U.S.A.)	Ice Cream
Snacks	
Fantasyland Pretzel Stand (Storybook Circus)	Pretzels
Liberty Square Market (Liberty Square)	Fresh Fruit
Sleepy Hollow	Waffles
Meals	
Be Our Guest (Fantasyland)	Sandwiches
Casey's Corner (Main Street U.S.A.)	Hot Dogs
Columbia Harbour House (Liberty Square)	Chicken Nuggets & Mac 'n Cheese
Jungle Skipper Canteen (Adventureland)	Steak & Crispy Chicken
Pecos Bill Café (Frontierland)	Fajitas, Tacos & Southwest Burgers
Pinocchio's Village Haus (Fantasyland)	Pizza
Frontierland Turkey Leg Cart (Frontierland)	Turkey Legs
Cosmic Ray's Starlight Café (Tomorrowland)	Burgers & Sandwiches

Epcot

Restaurant (Location)	Food Type
Sweets	
Karamell-Küche (Germany)	Candy
L'Artisan des Glaces (France)	Ice Cream
Les Halles Boulangerie Patisserie (France)	Cakes & Pastries
Kringla Bakeri Og Kafe	Cakes & Pastries
Snacks	
Sunshine Seasons (The Land)	Fruit & Cakes
Meals	
Electric Umbrella (Future World)	Hamburgers and Flatbread Pizza
Space 220	American Fare
Sunshine Seasons (The Land)	Chicken Nuggets & Mac 'n Cheese
Les Halles Boulangerie Patisserie (France)	Sandwiches
Sunshine Seasons (The Land)	Peanut Butter & Jelly Sandwiches
Via Napoli (Italy)	Pizza
Lotus Blossom Café (China)	Egg Rolls
Tutto Italia (Italy)	Spaghetti and Pizza
Via Napoli (Italy	Pizza
La Cantina de San Ángel (México)	Tacos
Yorkshire County Fish Shop (UK)	Fish 'n Chips

Hollywood Studios

Restaurant (Location)	Food Type
Sweets	
Hollywood Scoops	Ice Cream
Oasis Canteen	Funnel Cakes
Sweet Spells	Caramel Apples & Candies
Tune-In Lounge	Peanut Butter & Jelly Milkshakes
Min and Bill's Dockside Diner	Chocolate Milkshakes
Woody's Lunch Box	Root Beer Floats & Tarts
Snacks	
Anaheim Produce (Sunset Ranch Market)	Fresh Fruit
Baseline Tap House	Pretzels & Cheese
Milk Stand	Blue & Green (Alien!) Milk
Meals	
Backlot Express	Hamburgers
Fairfax Fare	Hot Dog
Hollywood & Vine	Macaroni & Cheese
Studio Catering Co.	Peanut Butter & Jelly Sandwiches
PizzeRizzo	Pizza
Mama Melrose's Ristorante Italiano	Pizza and Spaghetti
Toluca Legs Turkey Co.	Turkey Legs
Ronto Roasters	Wraps
Rosie's All-American Café	Veggie Burgers
Roundup Rodeo BBQ	BBQ Ribs & Chicken
Woody's Lunch Box	Sandwiches

Animal Kingdom

Store (Location)	Food Type
Sweets	
Dino Bite Snacks	Ice Cream
Kusafiri Coffee Shop and Bakery	Cinnamon Rolls & Cookies
Anandapur Ice Cream Truck	Ice Cream
Zuri's Sweets Shop	Candies
Snacks	
Harambe Fruit Market	Fresh Fruit
Meals	
Eight Spoon Café	Mac 'n Cheese
Flame Tree Barbeque	BBQ Ribs & Turkey Legs
Restaurantosaurus	Hamburgers, Hot Dogs & Chicken Nuggets
Yak and Yeti	Egg Rolls
Rainforest Café	Sandwiches, Hamburgers & Pizza
Pizzafari	Pizza
Satu'li Canteen	Quesadillas & Cheeseburger Pods

Food Allergies

If you, or someone in your family, has food allergies, you can ask for an Allergy Friendly menu at every Quick Service location. You can order from that menu, or even ask to speak to a manager who will help you make safe, allergy-free food choices.

Hotel Dining

There's plenty of *nosh* (food) at the Disney hotels! Keep in mind - while all of the restaurants located inside the parks allow for "park casual dress," the dress code for certain Resort Restaurants may call for you to dress up a bit nicer!

One really nice restaurant is the California Grill, located at the tip top of Disney's Contemporary Resort.

This is where you can get great views of the Magic Kingdom; you can see the fireworks show if you're there at the right time!

For an even fancier evening, the premier Disney World restaurant is Victoria and Albert's in Disney's Grand Floridian Resort. It's considered one of the best restaurants in all of Florida (but you have to be at least 10 years old to dine there)!

Other nice restaurants (called Signature Dining) worth checking out are Jiko at Disney's Animal Kingdom Lodge; Flying Fish at Disney's Boardwalk; and Yachtsman Steakhouse at Disney's Yacht Club Resort.

If you are looking for something a little more casual, try Boatwrights at Disney's Port Orleans Riverside Resort; Beaches & Cream Soda Shop (an old-fashioned ice cream shop!) at Disney's Beach Club Resort; 'Ohana at Disney's Polynesian Village Resort; or Olivia's Cafe at Disney's Old Key West Resort. Each of these eateries has a cool atmosphere with great food, and you get the chance to check out the neat resort properties!

Dinner reservations are usually required at all of these restaurants, so have an adult book early on the My Disney Experience app or through the *disneyworld.disney.go.com/dining/* website!

Character Dining

Character Dining is a big deal. It's a great way to meet Mickey and the gang, your favorite princesses and more without the wait - they come to meet you!

While there are character restaurants inside the parks, you might find it's even better to attend character meals at the hotels!

Try to do it on a day you don't plan to go to the parks. Your family has a more relaxed time because you're not rushed to get back to rides.

Chef Mickey presides over his namesake restaurant at Disney's Contemporary Resort - however, this restaurant is very busy and can feel kind of rushed.

Aside from Chef Mickey's, the other resort locations offer a less rushed environment, such as the Topolino's Terrace breakfast buffet at the Riviera Resort. Aspiring princesses can even meet royal characters each morning at the Garden View Tea Room in Disney's Grand Floridian. Visit any of these restaurants to get your character fix (reservations required!):

- 1900 Park Faire (Grand Floridian) - Alice, Mary Poppins and Friends
- Chef Mickey's (Contemporary) - Mickey and Friends
- Disney's Perfectly Princess Tea (Grand Floridian) - Princess Aurora and Friends (Breakfast Only)

- 'Ohana (Polynesian Village) - Lilo & Stitch (Breakfast Only); Island Entertainers (Dinner Only)
- Ravello (Four Seasons) - Goofy and Friends (Breakfast Only)
- Storybook Dining at Artist Point (Wilderness Lodge) - Snow White and Friends (Dinner Only)
- Topolino's Terrace (Riviera) - Mickey and Friends (Breakfast Only)
- Trattoria al Forno (Boardwalk) - Royal Couples (Breakfast Only)

Dinner Show

The Hoop-Dee-Doo Musical Revue takes character dining to a whole other level - and kids love it!

Watch as silly cowboys and cowgirls joke, dance, and sing away, all while you enjoy a tasty meal!

This dinner show is held at Disney's Fort Wilderness Campground, which has tons of other fun stuff that kids love.

Go early to see horses or ride on a wagon. You can even try a little fishing with your folks!

Find the Disney Princesses

N	B	L	A	A	L	M	U	N	N	A	B	U	R
H	E	T	A	U	R	T	L	W	P	E	N	P	L
U	A	I	R	R	E	L	S	R	S	I	A	O	R
R	A	A	I	O	A	I	E	A	I	L	L	C	N
A	B	N	L	R	S	N	N	D	L	E	U	A	A
P	E	A	A	A	I	N	C	E	D	R	M	H	R
U	L	P	A	N	A	M	R	A	L	D	R	O	L
N	L	E	R	E	I	E	M	O	A	N	A	N	O
Z	E	M	I	E	D	I	R	N	R	H	T	T	I
E	U	E	N	N	M	L	U	A	P	N	A	A	E
L	L	E	I	J	A	S	M	I	N	E	J	S	N
J	J	C	L	I	O	A	R	I	E	L	N	N	B
N	E	T	I	H	W	W	O	N	S	A	A	A	E
I	I	A	D	I	R	E	M	R	T	M	O	A	E

AURORA
ARIEL
CINDERELLA
SNOW WHITE
JASMINE
MULAN
TIANA
MERIDA
POCAHONTAS
BELLE
MOANA
RAPUNZEL

Let's Stay at a Disney Hotel!

Walt Disney World Resorts (Hotels)

Disney calls its hotels *resorts*, because there is so much to do at each of the 31 Disney-owned ones they have in Disney World.

Some properties have more than one hotel with the same theme. There are a total of 21 completely unique, themed hotel properties. That's a lot to choose from!

What do we mean by themes? Think of it this way: one property transports you to turn-of-the-century New Orleans, while another takes you to the wilds of Africa — complete with live animals!

There is something to interest everyone and each type of family. There are even different amenities and price ranges to match your family's size and unique needs.

All of the resorts have great pools; some have water slides and hot tubs to soak in after walking around all day. Many resorts also offer free nighttime movies and marshmallows!

Several of the resorts have supervised programs just for kids, where you can get away from your parents for a few hours and have fun with many activities!

Pick up an Activity Guide from the Front Desk of whatever property you're staying in to see all the amazing things you can do.

Disney classifies its resorts into different categories: **Deluxe, Moderate, Value** and **Campground.**

Deluxe is the most luxurious, meaning the nicest beds, softest pillows, great lighting in the rooms and even the nicest toilet paper! These resorts also have amazing pool areas, complete with water-slides and hot tubs.

If you're into fitness, the Deluxe resorts even have Gyms, though who needs the extra exercise with all of the walking around the parks?

You may be more interested in some pampering at a spa - found almost exclusively at Deluxe properties.

Moderate hotels also have awesome pools with water slides and hot tubs. The beds, pillows, lighting and toilet paper aren't quite as nice as the Deluxe Resorts, but they're still good.

Value Resorts focus on fun for families on a budget. They have neat stuff to look at and great pools and places to play. What they don't have are water sildes or hot tubs. They also have less options for dining than the other categories, although you can find great food courts at each one.

Disney World only has one **Campground** property. If you like camping, they have RV pads and hookups, places to pitch a tent and even cabins to rent! The rest of the amenities are on-par with the Moderate Resorts.

Some families want to splurge on a once-in-a-lifetime vacation, while others return year-after-year and want to stay on a strict budget. No matter which resort you choose, you can be assured there will be tons of fun and frolicking.

Disney imagineers came up with amazing designs and details for each resort, and every one has a very cool swimming pool (or two)!

Staying on Disney property keeps you just a few minutes away from all the action. This is because all Disney resorts include bus transportation (and a few have boat, monorail or even sky gondola options!)

to all four theme parks, Disney Springs, Typhoon Lagoon and Blizzard Beach.

There are so many different rooms. In fact, there are 35,969 rooms in total (if you include the non-Disney ones on-property).

It would take you over 98 years to stay in a different room each night!

Even if you are staying at one resort, you can visit any of the others to check them out, eat a meal, watch a nighttime movie or more!

Forget the alarm clock. Have your parents call the front desk to schedule a wake-up call for an early-morning phone call directly from one of the characters. It might be Mickey Mouse, but if he is busy, he might ask Stitch or another buddy to make the call.

Kid's Tip!

Watch the tourist channel on Disney Resort TV. It shows an exciting preview of some of the amazing fun you can find throughout Walt Disney World.

Water Transportation

Friendship Boats are what Disney calls the ferries that run between Epcot and Disney's Hollywood Studios parks. Friendship Boats are also found at Disney Springs - they're often transporting guests from there to Old Key West, Saratoga Springs or Disney's two Port Orleans Resorts.

The boats from Disney's Hollywood Studios to Epcot also make stops at the following hotels:

Disney's Boardwalk Inn

Disney's Yacht Club

Disney's Beach Club

Walt Disney World Swan and Dolphin hotels (not technically Disney resorts, but really close to the action!)

Magic Kingdom Area Resorts

Contemporary (Deluxe Resort)

The Contemporary was the first resort built at Walt Disney World. The name means "modern," which reflected its aesthetic (look) when it was built way back in 1971. How many years ago was that?

It's considered a Deluxe Resort for its luxurious accommodations throughout all 14-floors.

Remember, Deluxe Resorts are all luxurious and comfortable with the softest pillows and the plushest toilet paper!

Even though the Contemporary is the oldest resort… it's still one of the coolest and most convenient!

The Contemporary is home to Chef Mickey's restaurant - one of the most popular character-dining restaurants. Expect to see the chef himself bustling through the dining room and greeting his guests!

The monorail travels right through the inside of the Contemporary Resort on its special track! You can hop off and on at any time for a trip to the Magic Kingdom, the other two Magic Kingdom hotels and the Transportation and Ticket Center (where you can transfer to another monorail that takes you to Epcot)!

This resort is located right on the lake. You can jump on a boat to the Magic Kingdom. Another boat goes to the Wilderness Lodge or Fort Wilderness Campground to explore.

If you're really adventurous, your family can even rent a boat and drive it around the lake!

Look for the 90-foot tall (9 stories high!) mural in the center of the building. The colorful pictures include animals and young children. The mural was created by Disney artist, Mary Blair. She is considered a *Disney Legend*, because she also designed "*it's a Small World*."

Polynesian Village (Deluxe Resort)

The Polynesian is another Deluxe Resort. It brings a South Seas vibe to the Seven Seas Lagoon, with its tribal art. Look for tiki torches all around and a volcano swimming pool!

The Polynesian is a tropical island paradise. Everyone enjoys chilling in the authentic island theme.

If you're into wearing leis (necklaces made from flowers), flip flops and aloha shirts - this is the spot to do it! You can even stay in a Disney Vacation Club bungalow that sits on stilts out in the Seven Seas Lagoon!

The Polynesian has a huge pool area that is fitting for an island *motif* (theme), complete with a volcano that's actually a water slide!

It sits right next to a real sand beach where you can play volleyball or curl up on a hammock to watch the sun go down. (There is no swimming in the lake, however. Splashing around is limited to the pools.)

Talk to your parents about packing a family picnic dinner to enjoy on the beach, while watching the evening fireworks from across the pond! (The show's music is piped into the resort and it plays on speakers all around you.) Disney even shows movies and has marshmallows to roast (for free!) every night on the beach.

If you get hungry, Kona Kafe and 'Ohana have great tasting food. ('Ohana means family in the Hawaiian language.) Make sure you get reservations for the restaurant named 'Ohana early. It's one of the most popular places to eat at Disney World. That's because you can meet Lilo

Facts about the Monorail

Do you want to learn more about the monorail?

The monorail is part of the free transportation system at Walt Disney World. It currently operates 12 *Mark VI Monorail* trains, taking passengers between the TTC and either the Magic Kingdom or Epcot.

"Mono" means single or one. That's because the monorail only runs on a track that has a single rail, unlike most trains that have two rails. What makes it even more fun is that it travels on a railway that is high in the sky above everyone!

When Disney World opened in 1971, the monorail was a state-of-the art train system. It may seem a little old-fashioned now, but they're actually in the process of making it super high-tech and modern.

What do you think it will look like in 10 years? We can only imagine!

There are three separate monorail tracks, which take you to different destinations: Resort, Express and Epcot.

The Resort Line connects the Magic Kingdom with three hotels:

- Contemporary
- Polynesian
- Grand Floridian

The Express Line bypasses the resorts, making a non-stop, direct run between the Magic Kingdom and the Ticket and Transportation Center. That's where most people who drive to the Magic Kingdom park, but it gets its name because you can get transportation to anywhere in Disney from it!

The Epcot Line runs between Epcot and the Ticket and Transportation Center.

Sadly, no monorail tracks were built to go to Hollywood Studios or Animal Kingdom. Hollywood Studios has a really cool "Skyliner" gondola transportation system, though. It is awesome!

Trivia:

Did you know each Disney World monorail train has a name?

Train color = name

Red	Rose	Chrome	Bullet (Shine)
Orange	Florida	Peach	Georgia
Green	Katy	Gold	Alaska
Lime	Key	Coral	Reef
Black	Jack	Teal	Austin *In loving memory
Blue	Gem	Purple	Lavender (retired)
Yellow	Daisy	Pink	Valentine (retired)

& Stitch there during breakfast or watch island entertainers there during dinner. Who wouldn't want to eat here?!

For a quick snack, belly up to the Pineapple Lanai to try the world famous Dole Whip. It's the same tasty pineapple ice cream treat found at the Magic Kingdom. Yum!

The Polynesian is also home to the Spirit of Aloha dinner show, where hula and warrior-style dancers, along with fire-knife performers, entertain, while you stuff yourself with all-you-care-to-eat island favorites.

This is one of the "monorail hotels." You can take the monorail or a boat to the Magic Kingdom. It's also an easy walk to the Transportation and Ticket Center from the Polynesian to catch the monorail to Epcot.

Grand Floridian (Deluxe Resort)

The Grand Floridian is just that, completely grand! If you like to play dress-up or have tea parties, this is the place for you. Talk about a Deluxe Resort — this one's the most deluxe!

Think Victorian elegance. You might expect to see Mary Poppins coming down the grand staircase or a princess coming down the ornate glass elevator. It's that nice!

You can easily believe you're inside a Victorian-era mansion that soars 5-stories high, complete with chandeliers on the ceiling. The Victorian architectural style is from about a century ago — that would be the early 1900s. It's beautifully decorated and even has an elegant wedding pavilion that overlooks the shores of the Seven Seas Lagoon.

The hotel is home to Victoria & Albert's restaurant, which offers one of the finest dining experiences in all of Florida. This means it is really expensive and tasty food offered with great service. You really have to dress up nice to eat there, and they don't even allow kids under 10 in the restaurant!

The resort also has a spa - which may interest your parents, even though we know you're there to have fun and not get pampered!

If this all sounds a little stuffy, not to worry. The Grand Floridian welcomes children! They offer a lot of stuff for kids, even though it looks more formal than playful!

There is a large Alice in Wonderland-themed water play area, along with two awesome pools. (One is surrounded by beautiful roses, and the other has its own waterfall!)

They also offer storytelling and crafts. Look around to find sun rooms with comfortable chairs and a television set up to play classic Disney movies! Musicians and Bands play live music in the lobby - it's a lively place!

There are even more kid-friendly events. *Disney Perfectly Princess Tea Party* is a prim and proper, courtly tea party where you get to meet Disney princesses.

If you prefer a little more whimsy and fun, the Mad Hatter and Alice host the offbeat *Wonderland Tea Party*.

At Christmastime, check out the grand gingerbread house in the lobby! It's 16-feet

Disney Villains

Across

1. Tik Tok the crocodile ate Captain ________'s hand.

4. This sea witch wants King Triton's power.

7. She wants to make a coat from 101 Dalmatians.

9. Mufasa's jealous brother from The Lion King.

10. This man plots dastardly deeds against Belle's father, Maurice.

Down

1. No bug's life show would be complete without this nasty grasshopper.

2. Don't forget to invite this wicked fairy to your party.

3. Lady _________ is Cinderella's wicked stepmother.

5. Alice must outwit the Queen of _________.

6. Who holds power over Agrabah with a snake staff?

8. The ________ Queen was the original Disney villain.

*Answers on Page 211

tall and made with REAL gingerbread. The house is so big, the inside of it is a retail store where you can buy the tasty stuff (coated in chocolate). Yum!!!

This is the third (and final) "monorail hotel" (along with Contemporary and Polynesian Village). You can take either the monorail or a boat to the Magic Kingdom.

Wilderness Lodge (Deluxe Resort)

Take a trip out West!

You can easily believe you've stepped into a grand mountain lodge within Yellowstone National Park at the The Wilderness Lodge. There is even an actual, erupting water geyser that spouts high into the air hourly, just like Old Faithful!

If that's not enough to excite you, flowing hot springs run through the lobby and outdoors, over the waterfall. They run directly into the super fun and huge swimming pool and keep it heated.

Storybook Dining at Artist Point is a pretty fancy restaurant that serves Pacific-Northwest cuisine (steaks and seafood). You can meet some really rare characters while you eat there, including Snow White, the Seven Dwarfs and even the Evil Queen!

The kid-favorite restaurant is Whispering Canyon Café. It delights anyone just looking for a little fun while eating a meal!

The Wilderness Lodge is best known for its rustic, mountain retreat look. It's like ski lodges found at a national parks. It looks like a giant, log-mansion. Inside the main lobby, you can sit around the community fireplace that burns year 'round.

Pay attention to all the decorative details, too. Can you spot the Native American totem poles?

Fort Wilderness Campground is just next door. You can take about a 20-minute wilderness hike through the woods to get there. Look closely for real, live deer and other small forest animals along the way!

There are all sorts of fun activities surrounding Wilderness Lodge.

A fun activity to try is bicycling. You can bring your own or rent one there. You can even take a boat to the campground or the Contemporary across the lake.

Be sure to check out the "Proterozoic Fossils and Minerals" exhibit – use the key to identify rocky strata represented in the fireplace construction.

Maybe you want to take a self-guided Hidden Mickey Tour at Wilderness Lodge. This is a fan favorite. Pick up a map from the front desk! Turn it into a contest to see how many Hidden Mickeys you can locate.

The best way to get to Epcot, Hollywood Studios and Animal Kingdom from this resort is by bus. There's also a boat that ferries guests to the Magic Kingdom and back from a dock located below the pool area.

Fort Wilderness (Campground/ Moderate Resort)

You can also spend the night in a camper, Recreational Vehicle (RV) or tent at the Wooded campgrounds called Fort Wilderness! If you don't have a camper, there are great cabins to rent.

There's plenty to do here; spend time on the canals, mosey along the peaceful walking trails, take a wagon ride or visit the pony farm! You can even take a horse ride on a trail through the forest.

Chip 'n' Dale visit each evening for a campfire sing-along and marshmallow roast. (Even if you're not staying at the Campground, feel free to stop by and enjoy the show!)

Fort Wilderness is also home to the very popular western dinner show called *Hoop-Dee-Doo Musical Revue.* It costs quite a bit of money, but is a ton of fun. Get ready for a real hoedown!

Epcot and Hollywood Studios Area Resorts

If you plan to go to all four theme parks, you might want to stay in one of the three main Epcot and Hollywood Studios-area resorts. This is because they have a great, central location on Walt Disney World property (meaning you won't have to drive a long way to get anywhere).

The three most convenient of them are Boardwalk Inn, Yacht Club and Beach Club.

Two non-Disney hotels, Walt Disney World Swan and Dolphin, are found nearby and make a great alternative to the Disney-owned resorts.

Riviera and Caribbean Beach are also Epcot/Hollywood Studios resorts, though they're a little off the beaten path.

Technically, all of those hotels are Epcot resorts. There's a new resort opening that is the only actual Hollywood Studios resort. It's called Star Wars: Galactic Cruiser, and it may just be the coolest hotel in the world!

Kid's Tip!

Caribbean Beach is so big, it takes a long time to walk to the main pool area from some of the rooms. It can also take a long time to catch a bus to the parks if you're on the outer edges of the resort.

Ask your parents to reserve a room close to the pirate ship pool to make sure you're always close to the action!

Boardwalk Inn (Deluxe Resort)

Disney's Boardwalk Inn isn't just a hotel, it's a whole dining and entertainment area. The Boardwalk isn't nearly as big as Disney Springs, but there is a lot to do. It sits on a lake between Epcot and Hollywood Studios. In fact, you can easily walk to either of the two parks from the Boardwalk!

While the Boardwalk is probably the most convenient to both parks, there are other easy to walk to hotels around the lake: Disney's Yacht and Beach Club Resorts and Walt Disney World Swan and Dolphin hotels. If you've had enough walking, there are also boats between all those resorts and both theme parks.

The Boardwalk Inn has the old-fashioned look of the Atlantic City boardwalk (in the East Coast state of New Jersey) at the turn of the 20th century (early 1900s). Fun carnival games, including a basketball hoop toss, and other forms of entertainment stretch down the promenade. There's even a caricature stand where you can have an artist make a silly drawing of you as a souvenir.

Did you know? Boardwalks get their names because the path is made from actual wooden planks!

When you get hungry, there are plenty of snack stands along the Boardwalk, including the American (and kid) favorite, funnel cakes!

There are several great restaurants too! Choose from the tasty Trattoria al Forno (with a royal couples character meal for breakfast!), Flying Fish Café, ESPN restaurant and more.

Your parents even have special places of their own where kids aren't allowed, such as the adults-only Atlantic Dance nightclub and Jellyrolls, a dueling piano bar.

Travel around the Boardwalk in a fun way by renting bicycle-vehicles (called surreys) big enough for a small family (up to four people)!

The hotel itself has a giant pool that looks like an old-fashioned amusement park. What fun!

Did you know? There is a crystal globe "time capsule" in the main building that is scheduled to be opened on the 50th anniversary of WDW — not too far away, on October 1, 2021.

Yacht and Beach Club (Deluxe Resorts)

Disney's Yacht & Beach Club are two resorts that share the most popular pool area on all of Disney property: Stormalong Bay.

What makes it so amazing? The pool has sand covering the bottom! This makes it feel like you're really at the beach. There is even a pirate ship water slide!

In fact, the three lagoons that make up the pool area are so large, most people staying here don't bother with the waterparks.

The hotels are themed to go together like peas and carrots! The Yacht Club uses lots of dark wood for its nautical (boat) theme. It's supposed to look like elegant New England seashore hotels from the 1880s. The Beach Club is light and airy, giving it a laid back beachfront vibe.

Just like the Boardwalk Inn, you can easily take a boat or walk to both Hollywood Studios or Epcot's International Gateway entrance from each resort.

Kid's Tip!

The International Gateway is the back entrance into Epcot. You enter right in the heart of World Showcase.

This is really convenient if you just want to get dinner or watch the nighttime fireworks show.

It's also way faster to get back to your hotel from there if you're staying at the Boardwalk Inn, Beach or Yacht Club.

One of the absolute best places for kids to eat at Disney World is a small restaurant named Beaches and Cream. It's an old-fashioned ice cream parlor located right at the Beach Club. You can get tasty sandwiches, burgers, flavored sodas and a giant ice cream treat called the kitchen sink! There is even a completely free Jukebox that plays records from the 1950s and 60s!

If seafood is what you crave, there's a really popular buffet called Cape May that has *all-you-can-eat* crab legs. For really special occasions (like your parents' anniversary), see if you can get a reservation at the really fancy Yachtsman Steakhouse.

The best thing about Disney's Boardwalk, Beach and Yacht Club Resorts is that they are all within walking distance to both Epcot and Hollywood Studios. (Take your sneakers for the 15 to 20 minute stroll. You can also take a boat!)

Star Wars: Galactic Cruiser

You and your family can stay in a docked spaceship at this Star Wars-themed hotel. Hang out on the ship's bridge and sleep at night in your very own launch pod. You won't beleive your eyes when you see it!

Disney plans to offer special Star Wars vacation packages you can only get if you stay here.

Caribbean Beach (Moderate Resort)

Have you always wanted to visit a Caribbean island?

You won't need to after staying at this resort! There's a huge lake with lots of sandy beaches. Every building is bright, colorful and cheery.

As much as kids love the quirky look of the place, they love the pool even more.

There's a huge water play area with a giant pirate ship - and it's just for kids!

The main pool also has a fun water slide, waterfalls and water canyons. There are six more quiet pools around the rest of the resort. It's massive!

Remember, the Caribbean is known for all the pirates who used to sail those seas.

Your parents can reserve a pirate-themed room, complete with pirate ship beds! (Keep in mind these rooms cost a bit more and have limited availability, so you might not be able to get one.)

There's a great food court to eat at. Remember to order a kids meal. It comes with a bucket and shovel to go outside and play in the sand!

You can use the bus system to get to each theme park from Caribbean Beach, but there's a much cooler way to get to Hollywood Studios and Epcot.

The gondola system, called the *Disney Skyliner*, allows guests to travel in the sky from Caribbean Beach to Epcot and Hollywood Studios!

Riviera (Deluxe Resort)

Experience all the luxury of a European resort right in the middle of Florida! Riviera Resort is a Deluxe Villa Resort, so it's got a lot to appeal to kids and adults.

Walt Disney loved the continent of Europe, bringing many European stories to life in his movies and theme parks. This resort makes guests feel like they're visiting the European Riviera.

This hotel is inspired by Mediterranean and European art and architecture with a bit of fairytale thrown in. Maybe your inner artist will be inspired as you relax and dine in a rooftop restaurant, all while enjoying amazing views.

The Riviera is within walking distance to Caribbean Beach. Just like that resort, you can hop on the Skyliner for a quick trip to Epcot or Hollywood Studios. Bus transportation is available to everywhere else on Disney property.

Swan & Dolphin (Deluxe Resorts)

Even though the Swan and Dolphin hotels aren't Disney hotels, your family might like staying there. They are located right next to Disney's Boardwalk and have most of the same perks as Disney hotels.

They're Deluxe Resorts (meaning they are really nice), but you can sometimes find rooms there for cheaper than Disney's official Deluxe Resorts!

Both hotels make up one huge resort area with a shared pool (like Disney's Yacht and Beach Club).

Each hotel is a huge tower with immense statutes on top of swans and dolphins. You might get a little confused when you see them, though. That's because the statue is of a dolphin fish, not the smart mammal that we call a dolphin!

These hotels are known for having great places to eat. Many of them are really nice, expensive restaurants, such as *Todd English's bluezoo* and *Shula's Steak House* at the Dolphin or *Il Mulino New York Trattoria* at the Swan.

Restaurants kids really like include *The Fountain* (ice cream!) and *Mediterranean Market* at the Dolphin, as well as *Garden Grove Cafe* at the Swan.

Both Epcot and Hollywood Studios are a short walk from the Swan & Dolphin. It's a lot more fun to take a boat, though!

It is just across the lake from Disney's Boardwalk and all of those great activities.

There are over 250 swan and dolphin statues across the property, small and large. Try to find them all!

Disney Springs Area Resorts

Saratoga Springs (Deluxe Resort)

Before the Disney parks were built, Americans already loved to vacation. One of America's earliest vacation destinations was Saratoga Springs in upstate New York, outside the *Big Apple* (New York City's nickname).

Disney's Saratoga Springs resort is made to feel just like the original upon which it is modeled. It looks like it was build in the late 1800s, with Victorian-style cottages lining the streets and horse-racing motifs throughout.

There's a big lake with lots of flowers around it. This lake isn't just for show. You can bring a fishing rod and try for some catch-and-release fish! (That means you put the fish back after you catch it.)

There are a few pools on the property and a big water-play area. One of the pools comes with fountains that squirt and spray to keep kids cool!

Adults especially like this resort, because they can relax and get pampered at the full-service spa between long trips to the park.

Saratoga Springs is really convenient to Disney Springs. It's a quick jaunt across the pond, either by walking across one of two bridges or by a boat ride that takes less than 10 minutes.

There's also a nine-hole golf course called *Lake Buena Vista* golf course, and it's on the property!

Saratoga Springs is part of the Disney Vacation Club, but anybody can rent a room. Some of the rooms are big enough for an entire family and have full kitchens.

Treehouse Villas (Part of Saratoga Springs)

Have you always wanted your own treehouse? Well, you have never seen such fancy ones as these!

There's an actual forest oasis in the middle of the hustle and bustle. On it, are (real!) treehouse villas where your whole family can sleep high above the ground! The treehouses are built on top of pedestals along the lake and surrounded by trees. They're a kid's fantasy!

They're not small, either. There are three bedrooms, two bathrooms and a full kitchen. Each one is the size of a small house!

They're pretty costly, but the treehouses are perfect for larger families wanting peace and quiet. They are officially part of Saratoga Springs Resort, so you get to use all of those pools and restaurants when you return from nature!

Port Orleans - French Quarter (Moderate Resort)

Celebrate Mardis Gras every day at this festive resort - it's always a party at the French Quarter!

There's a place in New Orleans, Louisiana, called the French Quarter. This resort looks just like its namesake with really pretty buildings and fancy balconies overlooking real cobblestone streets.

The resort is pretty small compared to most of the Disney hotels, but there's a ton of stuff to do. If you're lucky, you might get a room that looks over Old Man River, which flows past.

Its swimming pool is another kid favorite. It features a fun, winding water slide that looks like a giant sea serpent. His name is Scales, but he looks a lot like Rex, the dragon king of New Orleans' parades.

Another pool is located just a short walk away at the resort's sister property, Port Orleans Riverside. You can get even more splashing-in-the-sun fun there. Since they're connected, you get to use the pools at both resorts!

There's one more thing you have to try, even if you don't stay at this resort. Near the food court here is the only place in Disney World that you can get a tasty beignet (a French word pronounced ben-yay). It's like a puffy French donut with yummy powdered sugar all over it.

Port Orleans - Riverside (Moderate Resort)

There is nothing but fun in Dixieland! This hotel used to be called Dixie Landings, because it has a Southern United States feel. Every building looks like a different southern mansion!

Old Man River runs straight through the resort. You can take a nice boat ride over to the French Quarter or all the way to Disney Springs.

Unlike the French Quarter, Riverside is huge - about four times the size of the French Quarter! It's a little more full-service and has a great table service restaurant with Cajun food.

You don't even need to leave the resort for entertainment. There's a funny and talented piano player named Ye Haa Bob who puts on a show at the River Roost Lounge most nights.

There are a total of six pools! The main one is especially cool with a water slide and tons of ways to splash and get splashed! Right next to it is a place to rent a fishing rod and try to catch a fish in the river!

You can spend hours just walking through this resort property. Try hiking on over to the French Quarter to eat a beignet!

Old Key West (Deluxe Resort)

Disney's Old Key West is the original Disney Vacation Club resort, but you don't have to be a member to stay here! It looks a lot like Key West in the Florida Keys, without the long drive to get there!

Everyone knows you go to Key West to simply relax and enjoy the palm trees and sunshine. That's what this resort is all about!

If your idea of fun is chilling by one of several pools or playing 18 holes of golf (on a real, professional golf course!), this is the resort for you. You won't get tired of the super slide at the main pool!

You have to eat sometime, and Olivia's Cafe is a favorite restaurant for kids and adults. They serve great food with a Caribbean vibe.

Did you know? Key West is the southernmost point in the continental United States. The city is only 90 miles from the country of Cuba! Continental means it's attached to the mainland continent that makes up most of the United States.

The 50th state admitted to the union includes the handful of islands that makes up Hawaii. It is located further south than Key West, but nowhere near the mainland!

Old Key West is just a boat ride away from Disney Springs. If you have a lot of energy to burn, you can take a really long walk along a wilderness path (that runs along the river). It eventually takes you to Disney Springs.

Animal Kingdom and ESPN World of Sports Area Resorts

Animal Kingdom Lodge (Deluxe Resort)

This Disney hotel has real, live animals roaming around! Get up-close-and-personal with the animals at Disney's Animal Kingdom Lodge!

The hotel is tucked away among trees in a natural wilderness environment. It seems really remote, but it's actually right next door to the Animal Kingdom theme park.

This Deluxe Resort is styled as a giant hut-style lodge, complete with thatched roofs and even a huge mud fireplace in the lobby.

Did you know? If the Animal Kingdom Lodge seems kind of similar in looks to the Wilderness Lodge, there's a good reason for that. It was designed by the same architectural company!

You can easily imagine stumbling across this place on safari in Africa. It is laid out in a horseshoe shape with many of its rooms looking out onto a 46-acre African *savannah*. (That's a flat, grassy plain.)

Animals roam free across the property! Spot giraffes, zebras, ostriches and other wildlife that is native to Africa. There are special places to see them throughout the resort, but if your parents rent a Savannah View room, you can view them directly from the balcony of your own hotel room! The animals usually get a little closer to the buildings in the morning, so look out your window first thing when you wake up.

The lodge is split into two giant buildings (and some smaller ones), which means there are two awesome pool areas you can play in! Water slides and water play areas are easy to find in the midst of the jungle.

If you love to eat (who doesn't?), the Animal Kingdom Lodge has great options for kids. You can find food you normally eat, but if you're adventurous, there are some spicy choices. That's because a lot of African cooking uses Indian spices and flavors!

Two kid favorites are *Jiko - The Cooking Place* and *Boma*. Both of them cater to families in a fun way, although *Jiko* is a more formal place (so dress nicely!).

Sanaa is a little quieter, but has great food. Try the naan bread. It's fresh from the oven and so tasty!

When you're done eating at night, head outside to sit around the fire. Better yet, go look for the animals. You won't be able to see them in the dark - unless you borrow a pair of night vision goggles! That's right! There is night vision viewing of animals at the lodge, and you don't even have to be staying there to try it. Just ask your parents to go there for an evening.

While this is the most convenient hotel to the Animal Kingdom park, it is pretty far from the others. You can catch a bus and get to the other parks within about 20 minutes.

Coronado Springs (Moderate Resort)

What a great place for an afternoon siesta (nap)!

If there is one thing you need to know about Coronado Springs, it's that the main pool has a giant pyramid!

Grand Mexican and Southwestern United States designs are what this resort is all about. (The Southwest United States includes areas from California through Texas, including Arizona and Nevada.)

The buildings look like they were created by hand from the clay ground, just like you would find in those areas. Did you know that adobe (clay) buildings have been common to home construction for thousands of years?

Did you know? Pyramids aren't just found in Egypt.

In Mexico and South America, the Mayans and Aztecs built large pyramids.

Many of them are still around. You can even visit some - if you can make it through the jungle!

The first thing to do when you get here is search for the main pool. Just look for the big pyramid! Of course, it also has an awesome slide. (It passes under a spitting jaguar!) There is a large sandbox next door to seek out hidden treasures.

Mexican food is always a kid favorite, and lots of it can be found at Coronado Springs! Don't worry, there is a kids' menu with other options if you want to choose something different.

Like the Animal Kingdom Lodge, Coronado Springs is very convenient to the Animal Kingdom park. You can reach that, as well as the other theme parks, by bus.

Art of Animation (Value Resort)

Most hotels are built with the entire family in mind. Disney's Art of Animation said, "Forget that!!! We're going to make a place that is just for the kids!"

It's a little different than most Walt Disney World resorts in that it offers more family-sized suites than any other resort. That's only part of what makes it so cool, though.

Each section of the resort is completely different with an awesome, immersive theme! Live out your favorite cartoons. The four animation-themed sections are:

- Cars
- Finding Nemo
- The Lion King
- The Little Mermaid

They packed this resort with enormous statues (some you can play on!) and artwork from these great Disney films. Be sure to check out the lobby walls and chandelier for more storyboard pictures!

Even the rooms make it feel like you're inside a cartoon!

Choose your favorite to stay in. Just remember, The Little Mermaid section is normal sized hotel rooms. All the others are family suites.

If all of that isn't enough, the main swimming pool has one of the coolest features ever. It plays music that you can only hear underwater!!! In fact, guests from Pop Century resort often try to come over and use it, but it's off limits if you're not staying at the Art of Animation!

They have high security to assure only resort guests are playing in the water. That way, it's never too busy for you to enjoy.

There are other pools, too. If you get tired of the main pool, try the kid favorite splash zone in the Finding Nemo section courtyard.

With all these great amenities, you will think this is a Deluxe Resort. But it's actually considered a Value Resort, which means it's a little more affordable for families on a tight budget.

You can take a bus to get to each theme park from Art of Animation. If you're a little more adventurous, try the gondola system, called the Skyliner, which allows you to travel in the sky from Art of Animation to Epcot and Hollywood Studios! (You read all about the Skyliner previously.)

Pop Century (Value Resort)

If you love retro, check out the Pop Century Resort! It pays tribute to the 1950s through 1990s, so your parents and grandparents will see lots of stuff that makes them smile. This resort is full of nostalgia (which means it reminds us and honors the era of the past).

Discover many of the things that made the last half of the 20th century special in the culture of the world. This includes film, animation and even iconic television characters and scenes.

There are huge, larger-than-life icons that are so much fun to discover - such as giant Mr. & Mrs. Potato Heads, a giant cell phone, a giant computer, an oversized Rubik's Cube and even a huge Big Wheel!

Each hotel building (called a wing) has a theme based on a particular time period.

Like each Value Resort, Pop Century has several pools, plus an interactive fountain to splash around in!

A bus transports guests to each theme park from Art of Animation. If you're a little more adventurous, try the Skyliner gondola system to travel from Pop Century to Epcot and Hollywood Studios!

Pop Century's Building Icons

Building Number: Room Numbers	Era	Main Icon
1: 1101 - 1472	1950s	Lady from *Lady and the Tramp*
2: 2101 - 2472	1950s	Jukebox
3: 3101 - 3472	1950s	Tramp from *Lady and the Tramp*
4: 4101 - 4472	1960s	Can of Play-Doh
5: 5101 - 5472	1960s	Mowgli and Baloo from *Jungle Book*
6: 6101 - 6472	1970s	Mickey Mouse Telephone
7: 7101 - 7472	1980s	Roger Rabbit
8: 8101 - 8472	1990s	Laptop Computer
9: 9101 - 9472	1980s	Sony Walkman Music Player
10: 0101 - 0472	1970s	Big Wheel

All-Star (Value Resorts)

The All-Star Resorts were the original Value Resorts at Disney World. They were made for families to have fun on a budget.

There are three completely different All-Star Resorts, each with its own theme: Music, Movies and Sports!

Just like Disney's Pop Century, there are giant icons throughout each resort. It's Awesome! (Going full-bore with design is what Disney does best!)

Look for giant musical instruments everywhere and even some enormous cowboy boots at the Music Resort. One of the pools features The Three Caballeros, the famous, musical bird trio featuring everyone's favorite duck!

Giant statues of Disney film characters, like Pongo the dalmatian or the 38-foot-tall Buzz Lightyear (almost four stories high!), can be found all over the Movies Resort.

See if you can spot some of your favorites!

Sports Resort icons include giant football helmets, tennis rackets, basketballs and more. There's even a huge football field to burn off a little energy!

Spotting these enormous icons is pretty easy - they're hard to miss!

Hidden Mickeys can be found everywhere around these resorts. It's a great time to go on a scavenger hunt to find each. (Hint: there's one in the main icon of each building complex.)

The All-Star Resorts are closest to ESPN World of Sports, so they're great to stay in if you have a sports event there. Buses get you to all the theme parks within about 20 minutes.

Puzzle Answers

Did you enjoy the puzzles in this book? We hope you solved all of them! If you need a little help, here are the answers to the crossword puzzles.

Animal Kingdom Favorites

Across

2. This type of big cat is found in Asia. Tiger
3. This type of big cat is found in Africa. Lion
5. A paleontologist digs up bones of what type of animal? Dinosaur
6. Known for its conservation efforts, Animal Kingdom opened on Earth Day in 1998.
7. Take a ride on this alien creature in Pandora. Banshee
9. The Tree of Life is the Animal Kingdom's park icon.
10. Come face to face with the Yeti (Abominable Snowman) while climbing the Forbidden Mountain.

Down

1. The glowing plants in Pandora are known as bioluminescent.
4. What mythical creature is found on some benches at Animal Kingdom? Dragon
8. Take a real African safari to see wild animals in Disney's Animal Kingdom

Disney Princesses

Across

2. Don't mess with this princess who has been to war. Mulan
4. Snow White was the first Disney princess.
5. This princess dreams of a life on land. Ariel
7. She knows how to get down and dirty with a mop. Cinderella
9. Don't cut her really long hair! Rapunzel

Down

1. She'll make you see the "Colors of the Wind." Pocahontas
3. The sea called out to this princess. Moana
5. She met her true love and prince, before she even knew she was a princess. Aurora
6. The only way to her heart is through a library. Belle
8. Only her sister, the Queen, could save her from a cold spell. Anna

Disney Trivia

Across

3. In what month did Walt Disney World open? October
5. Walt Disney World is about the same size as what city in California? San Francisco
7. What is "Yen Sid" (the name of the sorcerer in Fantasia) spelled backwards? Disney
8. In what month was Walt Disney born? December
9. Who was Walt Disney's favorite U.S. President? Lincoln
11. The first Walt Disney World theme park to open. Magic Kingdom

Down

1. Walt considered this Missouri city to be his home town. Marceline
2. Epcot stands for Experimental Prototype Community of Tomorrow.
4. Walt's brother, friend and business partner. Roy
6. The first Disney amusement park, opened in the 1950s. Disneyland
10. In which state is Walt Disney World located? Florida

Disney Villains

Across

1. Tik Tok the crocodile ate Captain Hook's hand.
4. This sea witch wants King Triton's power. Ursula
7. She wants to make a coat from 101 Dalmatians. Cruella
9. Mufasa's jealous brother from The Lion King. Scar
10. This man plots dastardly deeds against Belle's father, Maurice. Gaston

Down

1. No bug's life show would be complete without this nasty grasshopper. Hopper
2. Don't forget to invite this wicked fairy to your party. Maleficent
3. Lady Tremaine is Cinderella's wicked stepmother.
5. Alice must outwit the Queen of Hearts.
6. Who holds power over Agrabah with a snake staff? Jafar
8. TheEvil Queen was the original Disney villain.

Epcot Favorites

Across

4. Where can you find a pyramid in World Showcase? Mexico
6. Can you imagine a dragon like him? Figment
7. This ride will have you Soarin' high above the most famous places in the world.
8. This little rat will take you on an adventure through the streets of Paris. Remy
10. Epcot's park icon is a geodesic sphere.

Down

1. The American Adventure is the host pavilion for World Showcase.
2. Find a Beauty & The Beast topiary in the France Pavilion during the annual Flower & Garden Festival.
3. Create your own vehicle in a lab before setting out on this high speed ride. Test Track
5. Can you help Marlin and Dory find this little clownfish? Nemo
9. Queen Elsa cordially invites you to her ice palace in Arendelle.

Hollywood Studios Favorites

Across

3. Slinky Dog Dash takes you on a wild ride through Andy's backyard.
5. Learn how to race from Lightning McQueen.
7. Battle Darth Vader in the Jedi Training Academy.
9. Try to get passes to see this band at Rock 'n' Rollercoaster. Aerosmith
10. First name of the adventurer who shows you an "Epic Stunt Spectacular." Indiana

Down

1. Mickey and Minnie finally got their first theme park ride in Hollywood Studios.
2. Go on a high speed adventure in the famous Millennium Falcon.
4. The Tower of Terror is Walt Disney World's spookiest park icon.
6. These little aliens take you on a spin, hoping to be chosen by "The Claw."
8. Hollywood Studios used to be a working movie and television studio.

Magic Kingdom Favorites

Across

2. Meet Magician Mickey at his theater on on Main Street, U.S.A.
4. Big Thunder is the "wildest ride in the West!"
6. There are 999 spooks in the Haunted Mansion.
7. It's a Small World After All!
10. Captain Jack Sparrow stars in a pirate adventure.

Down

1. The Mad Hatter cordially invites you to take a spin at his Tea Party.
3. Fly high with Aladdin on a magic carpet in Adventureland.
5. Tom Sawyer had many adventures on an island in Frontierland.
8. What flying elephant takes you on a spin in Fantasyland? Dumbo
9. Who owns this castle where you're invited to Be Our Guest? Beast

Fun Things to Do

Across

3. Ride a boat across Seven Seas Lagoon.
5. Wave to Mickey and Minnie on top of their parade float.
7. The best ice cream bars to eat are shaped like Mickey Mouse!
8. Ride a fast roller coaster.
10. Let's go horse back riding at Fort Wilderness!

Down

1. If you want an autograph, get in line to meet a Disney Character.
2. The night sky lights up with Magic Kingdom's fireworks show.
4. See real animals in a safari.
6. Dress like a pirate and sing, "Yo Ho Ho."
9. Fantasia Gardens is a miniature golf course.

LIFEGUARD

Thank you for purchasing this guidebook. We appreciate our readers and value your support, as we strive for excellence in our materials.

If you enjoy our book, please have your parents **rate or review** it.

Like and follow us on Facebook:

www.facebook.com/groups/DisneyMadeEasyWDW

Share your love of Disney with us by joining our Facebook group:

Mickey's Not So Secret Disney World Fan Group

www.facebook.com/groups/mickeysfangroup

Printed in Great Britain
by Amazon